The Fell Pony

Shepherding in the Kentmere valley in the early 1950s. The Fell pony stallion Gipsy Prince carries a Swaledale ewe on the front of the saddle.

ALLEN BREED SERIES

The Fell Pony

Clive Richardson

J. A. Allen
London

British Library Cataloguing in Publication Data
Richardson, Clive
  The fell pony.
  1. Livestock: Ponies
  I. Title
  636.16

ISBN 0–85131–511–9

Published in Great Britain in 1990 by
J. A. Allen & Company Limited,
1 Lower Grosvenor Place
London SW1W 0EL

Series editor Elizabeth O'Beirne-Ranelagh
Book production Bill Ireson
Printed in Great Britain by The Bath Press, Avon

Contents

Front cover: Champion Fell pony, Bewcastle Bonny. Photo: M. G. Longsdon.

Endpapers: Fell stallion and mares on the breeding enclosure run by the Fell Pony Society from 1945 to 1975.

Acknowledgements

The author and publishers wish to thank the following people and institutions for providing photographs and the permission to publish them. Jennifer Buxton, for the drawings on pp. 2, 34, 59, 73 and 116; *Coventry Evening Telegraph* (p. 103); Miss P. Crossland; Charles Donaldson (pp. 46 and 84); K. G. Ettridge (pp. 11, 55, 92 and 94); Fell Pony Society; Steve Hogg (p. 26); Trevor Meeks (p. 110); Monty (p. 53); National Museum of Antiquities, Scotland (p. 18); Stuart Newsham (pp. 4 and 55); Alastair Penman (p. 27); *Preston Guardian* (p. 91); Paul Schmidt (pp. 104, 105); and Roy Wallis (pp. 60 and 112).

1 Introduction

The Fell pony has roamed the hills of northwest England for nearly 2000 years, but its history has been one of change and adaptation.

From early Roman times, when the breed originally evolved as a light draught animal, up to the present day when it is essentially an all-purpose ride and drive pony, versatility has been one of its great characteristics. By successfully adapting to the varied needs of man over the centuries, the Fell has succeeded in ensuring its survival without sacrificing breed type or character.

To the war-like Picts, the strong and tireless black ponies of northern England were ideal mounts for their raiding forays south of Hadrian's Wall. The Anglo-Saxons and Vikings used the Fell on the land to pull their simple ploughs and implements, and the Normans used it as a pack pony for carrying the wool clip from the shearing folds to the granges and abbeys for sorting prior to sale. Throughout, it was also a riding pony, carrying everyone from the early shepherds to the Abbot's professional 'wolvers' on their daily business.

The breed attained a position of great importance during the Industrial Revolution when its value as a pack animal was fully realised. Droves of these docile, strong and sure-footed ponies covered up to 240 miles a week, travelling on rough tracks and unmade roads at a steady walk, carrying coal, wool, iron-ore, farm produce, manufactured goods and other cargo. They were also used by the notorious smugglers who, under cover of darkness and with the ponies' feet wrapped in sacking to deaden any sound, carried contraband between the Cumberland ports and the market towns inland.

Large numbers of Fells were employed on the hill farms as general work animals. The Post Office used them in parts of Cumberland and Westmorland to deliver the mail, and as a driving pony they were popular with the tradesmen of the northern towns and cities.

The Fell's activities were not just confined to agriculture, commerce and industry for, in the nineteenth century, the breed achieved fame as a trotter. The sport had been practised since early times but came into prominence with the 'shepherds' meets', where matches between the shepherds' ponies and those of the Scottish cattle drovers who regularly passed through the Lake District made it a favourite entertainment. Among many notable 'mile in three minutes' trotters was Strawberry Girl, who won the Borough Stakes at Blackpool against all breeds in 1882.

The coming of the internal combustion engine and steam power on the land brought hard times for the breed, and in the early part of the twentieth century large numbers of Fell ponies were sold for slaughter. As the breed population was reduced, the future of the Fell pony looked uncertain.

The Fell Pony Society, which started as a sub-committee of the National Pony Society in 1898, encouraged breeders to register their stock and organised shows at which Board of Agriculture and War Office premiums were awarded. With financial support from such people as King George V and Mrs Heelis, better known as the children's authoress Beatrix Potter, the fortunes of the breed slowly recovered. By the 1950s when riding as a recreational activity began to take off, the Fell pony was no longer in danger of extinction and since then it has gone from strength to strength.

Under the patronage of HM The Queen, membership of the Society in the early 1990s is approaching a thousand with around 180 ponies being registered each year. Regional breed shows, a stallion show, an official sale of registered stock, performance trials and other activities are organised each year, and the Society issues its own stallion licences and publishes its own stud books. Far from being the regional breed it once was, there are now Fell pony studs in many parts of the country as well as ponies in a number of countries abroad.

Ridden and supreme champion at the 1989 Fell Pony Society breed show, Mrs Olwen Briant's Lunesdale Lucky Lady.

HM The Queen's team of Fell ponies driven by HRH The Duke of Edinburgh during the marathon phase of a combined driving event, 1984.

The uses of the Fell pony may have varied with the passing centuries but its appearance has altered little since post-Roman times. The present-day Fell is an ideal ride and drive animal, strong enough to carry a heavy adult yet not too big for a child to ride, an excellent jumper, economical to keep, and possessed of a very kind nature. The ever-increasing demand for Fells is evidence of the breed's success in adapting to the current needs of a discriminating equestrian market, and there is every reason to hope that the Fell pony will enjoy continuing success for many years to come.

2 The early origins of the Fell pony

Had anyone undertaken a survey of British pony breeds in the early to mid eighteenth century, their research would probably have revealed over twenty types of pony sufficiently distinct to be called breeds, that is reproducing their own particular form and characteristics with a certain degree of consistency. These breeds, most of which were extinct by the late nineteenth century, were all directly descended from a common ancestor, the wild European pony, which owed its origins to the Tarpan or prehistoric horse of Europe. From archaeological discoveries and early cave paintings of hunting scenes, we can piece together a picture of what these British ponies must have looked like. Small and coarse with large heads and probably dun in colour, they must have resembled their prehistoric ancestor more closely than did any of the later pony breeds they were to give rise to.

The wild European pony was not actually indigenous to the British Isles. It either migrated or was driven across the Channel, which was then a marshy stretch of water, by the nomadic hunters of the continent as long ago as 1500 BC. As these ponies gradually distributed to populate all parts of these islands, they came into contact with the variations in climate, soil and natural vegetation that were to produce the recognisable differences between the breeds.

From the handful of pony types which we know from archaeological excavations in various parts of the country existed in the first century AD, one type predominated in northern England and can be credited as the progenitor of the Fell pony. Standing at the very most about thirteen hands, brown, bay or dun in colour, its similarity to the Exmoor pony, which can be regarded as the oldest of our native breeds, can be attributed to the fact that the Exmoor is also the purest and therefore nearest to the original wild European type. Strong, vigorous and alert, these northern ponies roamed the vast expanse of moorland on either side of the Pennine watershed covering the present-day counties of Cumbria, Northumberland, Durham and Yorkshire and extending into Lancashire and the Scottish borders.

Although bleak and inhospitable, these moors for the most part grew coarse grasses or 'bents' as opposed to heathers, and the ponies travelled large distances in their small family groups led by a herd stallion seeking sufficient herbage on which to exist. The difficulty of finding enough to sustain life especially in the harsh winters, coupled with the extremes of climate for which this area is noted, ensured that only the fittest could survive the winters to breed in the spring. Packs of wolves which

Home territory: Fell mares from the Heltondale herd running out on the high ground above Haweswater.

followed the herds soon hunted down and killed any sick or weakly animals, and the human inhabitants of the area were known to hunt the wild ponies for meat whenever the opportunity arose. Hardiness and stamina developed as qualities to ensure survival. The type of terrain on which they lived also taught the ponies to be surefooted and nimble, and they developed the small, dense hoofs characteristic of breeds which have adapted to living in a mountainous habitat. Those breeds living in swampy lowlands tend to have large, flat hoofs.

The height to which these ponies grew was very much dictated by the quality of the vegetation they lived on. The coarse wiry grasses would not have supported ponies of more than thirteen hands and this ensured a height standardisation over many generations.

Excavation of Stone Age settlement sites have produced vast amounts of pony

Fell pony stallion, Heltondale Prince, foaled 1951. His appearance suggests the attributes necessary to survive on the northern hills. The Heltondale herd is one of the oldest studs still in existence.

bones in comparison to the skeletal remains of other animals, from which we can deduce that early hunters either had a preference for horsemeat or that wild ponies were more numerous and perhaps easier to catch than other animals. Even after hunting as a way of life was being replaced by crop farming and animal husbandry, the wild ponies – whose numbers had been drastically reduced by the invention of a lethal new hunting weapon in the bow and arrow – were not safe. The early stockbreeders were almost exclusively cattle men who now hunted the ponies not for meat but to eliminate the other large grass-eating animals from the available pasture land. As a result, the pony population in northern England was severely reduced and in some places may even have neared extinction. Those ponies left tended to exist in isolated pockets which encouraged in-breeding and consequently family or regional characteristics – the forerunner of distinguishing features between breeds.

Around 55 BC the expansion of the Roman Empire brought the first Romans to the shores of Britain. After a number of subsequent landings they settled in various parts of the country on a permanent basis, and their chroniclers give us the first accurate information we have about the early British horsemen and their ponies. Since the Bronze Age, ponies had been domesticated and used for pack work or to pull sledges laden with building materials, firewood or even animals killed for meat. Although the lack of roads limited the use of wheeled vehicles, there were some, for Julius Caesar wrote that he was not greatly impressed by the island or its inhabitants but described the war chariots used by the local Britons or Brigantes. They differed from the Roman chariot in being open at the front rather than at the back, and the wheels had long scythes projecting from the hubs so that when the chariot was driven at speed through enemy lines the effect was devastating. Another Roman, Cicero, wrote that there was little worth taking away from Britain except the chariots. The ponies that pulled these vehicles were always driven in pairs, which would support the other evidence that these ponies were not very large, and may also have explained why they were driven or used as pack animals but never ridden. Writing about the Roman invasion of Britain, Tacitus mentioned that the wives of the British charioteers watched the battles from carts positioned at the edge of the battlefields, which would suggest the use of the indigenous ponies in larger, more substantial vehicles as well.

In the north, despite initial victories, the supremacy of the Romans was constantly under threat from the war-like Picts who hailed from further north in what is now Scotland. Continual raids by the Picts made it difficult for the Romans to establish their position in the area, and in AD 120 Emperor Hadrian decreed that a vast wall should be built right across the country from the Solway to the mouth of the Tyne. The wall was to be built to a height of 15 feet with gates, sentry stands and fortifications at every mile point. As immense a project as the building of the wall required a huge workforce of both Romans and local people, augmented by bodies of foreign workers who, although originally employed as mercenaries on a contract basis, also doubled up as building operatives when required. During the Roman occupation of Britain there is evidence of foreign units from Hungary, Scythia, northern Spain, France and Belgium stationed along the wall and, more importantly as far as the Fell pony is concerned, there was at least one unit of Friesians.

In Roman times, Friesland was a province of some importance. Although now divided between the Netherlands and Germany, the inhabitants of the area still retain many of their old Friesian traditions including their dialect and costume. They were great seafarers and, as a consequence, great traders. Their deep-bodied, broad and roomy merchant ships were capable of carrying a far larger and heavier cargo than any of the more usual sea-going craft of the time, and the Friesians who sailed them were highly skilled and adventurous seamen. Place names like Friston in Lincolnshire testify to the extent of their travel and, at one time, there was a Friesian trading post in the city of York.

As merchants, the Friesians traded in a variety of goods including cloth, swords, metalwork and, most significantly, horses, and their merchant ships were among the few capable of carrying horses. As well as being traders in their own right, the Friesian seafarers were prepared to hire out their craft to others for the movement of either goods or personnel, and this aspect of their commercial enterprise was taken up by many, not least of whom were the Romans. It is highly probable that the Friesians may have played a major role in the Roman invasion of Britain simply by ferrying men, horses and equipment across the Channel.

The horses which the Friesians traded in were indigenous to their home area and belonged to one of the oldest breeds in Europe. The Friesian horses were large animals in comparison to other breeds of the time and grew to a height of around fifteen hands. Bred on the fertile sandy lowlands, these substantially built horses were invariably black in colour, and white markings were very rare. There is little reason to think that the present-day Friesian horse is much different from that of Roman times, and the breed is sufficiently distinctive to be easily recognised today. The head is finely chiselled and pony-like with small ears, and is carried on a well-shaped neck. The shoulder is well laid back and the body well sprung but rather shallow in many examples. The back is strong with powerful quarters. A particular

Friesian stallion showing the characteristics of the breed and the many similarities with the Fell pony.

feature is the legs, which carry much hair or feather, sometimes right up to the back of the knee, and the mane and tail are long and thick. One of its great qualities in early times as well as now is its docile and willing temperament which enables unskilled men to handle it. Renowned as a strong, tireless worker, its ability to thrive on poor-quality grazing was an additional bonus when it was exported from its homeland to many other countries, including Britain.

As well as a vast human workforce, the building of Hadrian's Wall also called for large numbers of horses to transport building materials, principally stone. From excavations of Roman camp sites in northern England and Scotland, we have evidence that there were several types of animals in the Roman stables at the time

Fell pony today still showing the Friesian influence. Clive Richardson, secretary of the Society from 1981 to 1990, competing at the 1984 Fell Pony Society breed show.

that the wall was built. One such site, Newstead in Roxburghshire, produced a wealth of bones from which could be identified a small pony not exceeding eleven hands and recognisable as a Shetland type; a slightly larger type up to twelve hands which would correspond with the wild pony of northern England, sometimes known as the Celtic pony; a twelve to thirteen hand pony with slender bones and unlikely to be capable of heavy haulage work; a thickset and longer-backed pony of the same size but with features like large hoofs which would suggest lowland or forest origins rather than moorland; an Arab type of horse measuring about fourteen hands; and a coarse-limbed animal of between fourteen and fifteen hands with a large head. This last type was almost certainly imported by the Romans as it existed in large numbers in central Europe and as far afield as India, and was the sort of horse used by the Germans as war horses and described by Tacitus as 'ugly and useless'.

Evidently, none of these types was ideally suited to the haulage work connected with the building of the wall. So much so, the Romans were compelled to look further afield for suitable animals and their search coincided with the employment of a cohort of auxiliaries – about 600 men – from Friesland. The system by which cohorts such as these were recruited was one much used by the Romans. The auxiliaries were employed for an agreed length of time, in this case probably until the wall was finished, and they were paid direct by the Army Paymaster. Quite often, the payment was a lump sum handed over at the end of the contract, but with long-term projects such as the wall payment was more usually made in small regular instalments. The Friesian auxiliaries brought their own horses with them and both men and horses were stationed at the fort of Rudchester on Hadrian's Wall.

By the fourth century, the auxiliaries had been replaced by federates, another kind of mercenary but not as closely integrated into the Roman military system. The federates were more like small private armies headed by their own chiefs. At the end of each campaigning season, the commander of each little army was handed a lump sum by the Army Paymaster and he was responsible for dividing it as he saw fit. Federates were responsible for supplying their own equipment and weapons as well as their own horses, and as there were several Friesian squadrons on the wall at this time it can be assumed that they were all mounted on Friesian horses specially imported for the purpose. One of these independent squadrons of Friesian cavalry, known as Prince Hnaufrid's Own, was stationed in the central section of the wall, and there was another mounted unit called the Cuneus Frisonum Aballavenis stationed at Burgh-by-Sands near the west coast. This second unit was also stationed for a time at Papcastle, near Cockermouth in Cumbria.

When the auxiliaries were disbanded with the option of re-enlisting as federates, many took their pay and returned home to Friesland. Employment as a mercenary was seen more as short-term work than as a career as such. In most cases it must have made more sense to sell their horses off to local buyers than trek them across country to a port on the east coast from whence they could be shipped back to Friesland. Consequently, a number of these impressive black horses came into the ownership of local people.

The Romans had seen Friesian horses in their native land and, being aware of their valuable qualities of strength and docility, saw them as being highly suitable for their requirements. Further shiploads of these horses were imported to supplement those already brought over by the traders and mercenaries. Although a total import figure of a thousand Friesian horses is frequently quoted, the number 'one thousand' is often used in a generic sense, rather like the number 'forty' in the Bible, to mean a large number and cannot be taken as accurate information. However, as the practice of gelding was virtually unknown at this time, and mares were hardly ever used for riding, driving or pack work – probably because they were usually either in foal or had a foal at foot – it can be assumed that the majority of the imports were stallions.

The Roman chronicler, Tacitus, whose observations on horseflesh generally were fairly critical, described the Friesian imports as 'slow, heavy and powerful', which compared to the Arabs and Barbs of the racetracks of his native Rome they may well have appeared to be. The Friesian horse was nevertheless a fast trotter with a long-reaching stride and the slight knee action characteristic of a breed capable of travelling over uneven ground. Low sweeping action would cause a horse to stumble and fall on anything but a smooth road, of which there were none until the advent of the Romans. In Britain, the only roads amounted to nothing more than dirt tracks littered with pot holes, which in a wet summer became difficult to negotiate and in winter were quite unusable.

One of the great qualities of the Friesian horse is its prepotency when used to improve other breeds. Not only does it pass on its strength, equable temperament and ability to live on poor-quality pasture, it also passes on its black coloration, making all breeds directly descended from the Friesian easy to recognise. Friesian merchants had conducted a busy trade with Norway for many generations and this included the sale of horses to their Norwegian allies. The Friesian imports interbred with the local ponies and the eventual result was the Gudbrandsdal, a strongly built black pony not unlike a Fell in many respects. Another similar breed is the Merens, a breed of draught pony found in the French Pyrenees, and again directly descended from Friesian imports. There was also a breed of black pony in Ireland, now extinct, but possessed of many characteristics of the Friesian horse which would seem clear proof that the ubiquitous Friesian traders had been there as well.

When mentioning the Friesian horse in this context, it should not be confused with the East Friesian horse, which was a much coarser draught type of animal produced from the same root stock but with the addition of Flemish and other blood.

Breeds develop slowly but by the time the Romans were well established in the north there must have been a definite type of dark-coloured pony, standing perhaps just over thirteen hands, bred within a local catchment area of the Roman wall. Bred from Friesian stallions and indigenous pony mares, the resulting progeny inherited the strength and quiet nature of the Friesian along with the hardiness, thriftiness and pony character of the north-country ponies. They were well able to stand the harsh climate and survive off the sparse vegetation of the region. Although most of the ponies were black, dark brown or bay, it is worth noting that dun, the primitive colour of the Tarpan, was also prevalent although it has now disappeared entirely from the Fell breed and was never recognised as an official breed colour. White markings were very rare. The size the ponies grew to was governed by the quality of the grazing and it is unlikely that a pony exceeding thirteen hands could have survived on moorland of the type found in the north. Had these ponies grazed the low sandy and fertile land of Friesland, it is quite possible that they may have grown as big as their Friesian ancestors. However, while size may have been lost, the substance of the Friesian was not. Subsequent generations of ponies followed the same consistent stamp, being powerfully built but active and free moving.

During the last two centuries of the Roman occupation of Britain, the constitution of the Roman forces, particularly in northern England, changed. There were fewer Romans and more recruits from local tribes employed in the defence and maintenance of Hadrian's vast wall, and large numbers of federates from other occupied countries were brought in. Many of the original Romans who had landed during the first years of the invasion had sons born to local women, and a new generation of Anglo-Romans were themselves stationed along the wall, and a gradual integration between the Romans and Britons was taking place. The highly efficient Roman military system was sufficiently well organised to cope with this infiltration by non-Romans at first; in fact it had little choice but to recruit outsiders if it was to maintain its numbers and keep the Picts and Irish at bay. In time, however, friction within the cosmopolitan Roman forces began to weaken the whole military machine. Frequent attacks on Gaul by Germans from across the Rhine necessitated the regular withdrawal of troops to go and restore the *status quo*, and more than one general with political ambitions required military support to stage his own particular *coup d'état*. As the power of Rome began slowly to decline, demoralisation within the ranks increased and, for the Romans on British soil, the beginning of the end was not far off.

For the Britons living near the wall and in the shadow of its protection, a mutual reliance had built up between them and their overlords. There was a considerable amount of trading between the two parties with local stockmen selling beef and pork to the Roman quartermasters and native ponies to the remount officers. At the main lookout posts and gates, busy outside markets flourished.

The reasons for the demise of the Romans in Britain and more especially in the north are not really clear, but certainly the rot had set in long before they were recalled to Rome to defend their besieged city from enemy attack. As far as the garrison stationed along Hadrian's Wall was concerned, although it was self-supporting to a large extent it still relied on Roman supply centres at York and Chester for certain supplies and, more importantly, financial support. When the rations and pay, which hitherto had arrived regularly, suddenly failed to materialise along the eastern sector of the wall, and no military orders were forthcoming either, the various commanders of the units stationed in that sector were presented with a very real problem. Supplies had never failed to reach the garrison before, thanks to the imperial posting service copied from the system used in Alexander the Great's time which in turn had been copied from that of the Persian Empire. This highly efficient posting system was used from one end of the Roman Empire to the other, and its success contributed largely to Roman military superiority as messages and orders could be relayed quickly and reliably over considerable distances. The unit commanders were therefore forced to assume that either an overwhelming enemy assault on headquarters had broken communication lines, or for some reason a major withdrawal of the legions had taken place leaving them on their own to cope as best they could. The result was confusion and internal bickering as to which of the commanders should take command. The Roman system of promotion, even in extenuating circumstances such as now faced them, was very complicated and, with no one obviously senior and entitled to take command of the situation, the dubious honour was eventually bestowed on one of the local British chieftains. Even though he had been an ally of the Romans and was consequently well versed in the mechanics of their military strategy, it was he who, as the strength of Roman power along the wall weakened, gave the command to evacuate the territory for which he had been made responsible.

The Roman regiments stationed along the west sector of the wall hung on a little longer and then either abandoned their posts and melted away into the local community or packed up and headed for mainland Europe to help defend Gaul from the Germans. Those who stayed followed what trades they had knowledge of or skill in. The mineral wealth of the north country had been known to the Romans who had begun to exploit it, using the same breed of draught ponies of Friesian descent they had used for the haulage work of building Hadrian's Wall and carting away the spoil from the wide ditch which ran parallel to the wall for its full length.

Although most of the foreign federates took what money they could get and went home when the Romans left, some also stayed on and settled in the north. Proof that some of the Friesian federates made their home here comes from place names like Frizington in Cumbria, which roughly translated from the Anglo-Saxon means 'Village of the sons of the Friesians'.

The departing Romans left a legacy of good roads which formed a national network connecting most places of any importance, and they introduced to Britain the civil engineering skills which enabled them to build bridges. Prior to the Roman occupation, road building had been restricted to the construction of narrow lines of flat stone flags called 'pack-trods' which were used by the strings of pack ponies that constituted the main form of overland transport at the time. In more isolated parts of the country, including much of the north, the 'trods' were innocent of even stone flags and were little more than single-width tracks worn out by a steady pack traffic. The Romans had learned the principles of road building from the Etruscans and used it to good effect in all the countries they had conquered. Although the roads were primarily for the movement of marching infantry, they encouraged an expansion in trade and a marked increase in the number of pack ponies travelling between centres of habitation.

The provision of good roads may have helped the merchants to move their wares but they did not instigate a shift from pack transport to wheeled vehicles. One reason was that with no good roads previously there was no tradition of using vehicles, and the few bullock wagons or heavy carts were cumbersome and slow. The absence throughout the ancient world of a suitable form of draught harness, especially a collar, meant that the tractive power of horses in draught was very limited, perhaps as little as two hundredweight (100 kg) being an average load for two horses in a two-wheeled cart. Lastly, the road surface paved with stone slabs was not ideal for wheeled vehicles which require a smooth continuous surface. Consequently, pack ponies were still the most usual form of transport and it is an indication of the general lack of demand for the Roman roads that they were allowed to fall into disrepair so quickly. Similarly, many of the bridges built for the benefit of marching columns of foot soldiers were allowed to crumble, as pack ponies could ford the rivers providing they were not too deep.

The early Fell pony type of animal made an ideal pack pony, as it was strong and surefooted, placid natured, and not too big to make loading and unloading difficult while still being well up to the weight of a full load. Unlike the small native ponies of pre-Roman times, the improved Fell type was large enough for a man to ride and was recognised as a dual purpose breed as such.

It is difficult to pin-point the stage in history when this Fell type could reasonably be called a breed, but by the fifth century it was well established and had adopted many of the features now characteristic of the present-day Fell pony. Although alien blood was inevitably introduced very occasionally right up to the twentieth century, the stamp of pony altered little with the passing of time, and the relatively confined breeding area for these ponies helped consolidate the type.

The weakening of defence forces along the Roman wall had been welcomed by the Picts, for whom the wall had been a hindrance but not the impenetrable boundary to their territory the Romans had hoped it would be. Pictish raiding parties had made frequent attacks on the fortified gates, or scaled the walls under cover of darkness, or even bribed the sentries on the gates to allow them to slip through. The Picts were primarily cattle thieves although they were not averse to taking other stock including horses, harvested crops or indeed anything that might be of value to them. Their raids varied from local sorties involving only a few men and taking two or three days, to large-scale raids employing large numbers of men and taking many months. For the latter they would travel hundreds of miles and there is evidence of Pictish raids as far south as Suffolk.

After the Romans had left Britain, there was considerably less resistance to the Picts and their raids began to cover an even wider area. To travel such distances, horses were a necessity and the Picts were fortunate in that their territory was large enough to give them access to a number of different types of pony ranging from the Shetland, whose native islands came under Pictish rule, to the larger mainland animals from which the Highland pony evolved, and much larger sorts evidently stolen from Roman camps or from settlements near the wall which had trading connections with the Romans. It was only a matter of time before descendants of the Friesian horses were driven off by the Picts to add to their already extensive herds. Impressed by their new acquisitions, they took them on raiding excursions to various

17

A Pictish stone carving, c. AD 800, showing a hunting scene. Notice that at least two of the ponies are moving laterally rather than trotting.

parts of the country. Ponies used in raids frequently got injured or lamed and would have been left behind as the raiders moved on, resulting in a distribution of the Fell type of pony which may have contributed to the rise of several new breeds.

One such breed was the Fen pony of East Anglia, a native pony very much on the lines of the Fell and obviously sharing common ancestry of Friesian horses and local pony blood. It is possible that Friesian stallions were imported direct to that part of the country by Friesian merchants or mercenaries as they had been to northern England, or it could be that Picts took ponies from the north down to the area and that these ponies were left to interbreed with local stock.

The semi-nomadic lifestyle of the Picts may also have been responsible for distributing the Friesian/Fell animals up into Scotland where they played a major role in the development of the now extinct Galloway pony, and into the Midlands where they formed the foundation stock for the Old English Black, a heavy draught horse which eventually was absorbed into and became the Shire horse.

Proof of the equestrian activities of the Picts can be found in their artistic representations of their horses, which make them unique as their contemporaries left no artistic records of their way of life. During the period between the end of Roman rule, which they never acknowledged, and their final amalgamation into the kingdom of the Scots, they developed a highly individual style of art which they expressed in a number of mediums. It is, however, their fine stone carvings which endured the intervening centuries to give us fascinating information about their horses. The best preserved examples are the memorial stones of chieftains and kings which are decorated with elaborate hunting and fighting scenes showing the deceased in a favourable light. A series of symbols are also incorporated in the designs to signify the rank and seniority of the chieftain, and these include such items as horse bits, tools likely to have been used by a blacksmith, and the terret ring from a chariot harness pad. Their inclusion would seem to signify the importance of horses to the Pictish people.

Of particular interest are the incredibly accurate representations of horses on the gravestones and memorial stones. They depict a wide variety of breeds and types, most of them being ridden although there are also examples of driven animals and even one pony being ridden sidesaddle by a Pictish princess. Significantly, ponies of Fell type are included in the carvings and if, like all other nations at the time, the Picts used only stallions for riding purposes, then as well as taking Fells out of the area their incursions back into the Fell territory must have brought stallions of fresh bloodlines. Obviously the prepotency of the Friesian had not been watered down in his descendants for the Fell seemed able to absorb occasional outcrosses without losing its own character and individuality.

Although the name 'Fell' was not to come into general use until the nineteenth century, the breed was fully formed and operational as an all-purpose riding and driving animal, pack pony, warhorse and hunter by the sixth and seventh century, and was ready for what was to be the most turbulent period in its history.

3 Establishing the breed under the Vikings and Normans

In the summer of AD 793, Norwegian pirates ransacked Holy Island off the coast of Northumberland, returning twelve months later to plunder a monastery at the mouth of the Wear. For the next three centuries, Viking seaborne expeditions increased both in number and size until few parts of the British Isles had escaped their hand and Scandinavian kings ruled the larger part of England, the north of Scotland including all the Scottish islands, the Isle of Man, north Wales, Anglesey and much of the Irish coastline. The Norse influence on our language and way of life was immense and Scandinavian settlers left a legacy of dialect words and place names all over northern England. It was, however, their contribution to the agriculture of the region that was of particular interest.

As little more than professional thieves, they stole most of their everyday requirements but, prior to permanent settlement overseas, were still compelled to undertake some farming, mainly arable, for winter supplies of oatmeal and rye from which they made bread, and barley from which they brewed ale. As arable farming needed able-bodied men, it had to be fitted in with the pirating season which took precedence and which began after the spring planting and finished well before harvest. Late frosts often hindered the spring ploughing, so once begun it had to proceed fast. Consequently, the Norsemen used horses instead of oxen for ploughing, a practice which was copied by the British and which in turn encouraged the wider use of horsepower in draught, under pack and on the land.

The Vikings also introduced the policy of gelding surplus colts, which was to have an enormous impact on the horse population of Britain. Although slow to be accepted at first, it was at least the first attempt at selective breeding and it made available a supply of geldings with a more suitable disposition for everyday work. Up until then, indiscriminate breeding by large numbers of stallions of inferior quality had done little to improve any of the British breeds, including the Fell.

Improvements in agriculture instigated by the Norse settlers led to increased hay crops and ultimately to better standards of horse feeding. Together with the first tentative steps being made in selective breeding, this brought significant benefits to all domesticated ponies.

In 1066, the Norwegian king led his Vikings to a great victory at Gate Fulford and

Five geldings, all sired by Packway Royal, on a Fell Pony Society pleasure ride. The practice of gelding was introduced by the Vikings.

was about to enter the city of York when the English king, Harold, defeated him miserably, only to turn south and be killed at Hastings defending his country from the Normans. Several ill-conceived and badly coordinated uprisings along the east coast failed to halt the Norman invasion and led instead to reprisals, the severity of which devastated the country. Settlements were ransacked, buildings burned or pulled down, crops destroyed and stock either killed or driven off, leaving a trail of dispersal, depopulation and starvation. Judicious distribution to Norman estates of land suitable for recultivation in places of strategic importance helped ensure no further uprisings, but much land was just left to waste.

Ironically the 'harrying of the North', as it was later known, was responsible for great advances in horse breeding and in the standardisation and improvement of the Fell pony. The reason lay in the shortcomings of the traditional system of keeping and breeding horses in Anglo-Saxon and medieval England.

The utilisation of the land belonging to each manor was arranged in concentric circles, with the arable land at the centre used not only for crops but also for sheep which grazed the corn stubble or those fields left fallow on the three-year rotation system favoured throughout medieval times. Next to this lay permanent meadow-land shut up for hay early in the spring and grazed by plough oxen or milch cows after the hay crop had been taken. Beyond this was common land grazed by store cattle or dry cows. Woodland bordering the common land had little agricultural use except for foraging pigs, and the moorland and upper slopes, which was very rough grazing, was where the horses and goats were kept. This was not because horses and goats did better on rough land in comparison to other stock, it was because they were capable of self-defence. Up until the fourteenth century, wolves were a real threat to livestock. Cattle were too slow to cope with attacks by wolves, and sheep were entirely defenceless, but both goats and ponies were resourceful enough to defend themselves and could be left in the care of the women and boys while the men tackled more pressing work.

Complete reliance on predators, the elements and the poor-quality grazing for selection may have ensured that all breeding stock was hardy and strong, but it did not guarantee standards of quality, size or conformation, and in-breeding was very common. The trouble lay in the abundance of stallions kept as breeding stock irrespective of value, and the fact that the practice of gelding learned from the Norsemen was slow to gain widespread acceptance.

The only horses kept within the settlements themselves were those used for riding or packwork. Riding as a means of transport was becoming more common, helped along by the Viking introductions of the stirrup and saddles of a more comfortable design. Previously, saddles had either been on the lines of a wooden packsaddle or had consisted of layers of padded cloths secured in place with a surcingle. In settlements of Anglian as opposed to Norse population, any riding animals would have been stallions as the riding of mares or geldings was regarded with disdain on account of prestige. Riding stallions were kept in an enclosure or 'close' in the centre of the village, as evidenced by place names like 'Stony Horse Close', meaning stallion enclosure, which are common throughout the north. The use of a 'close' meant that riding horses were readily available when required, and valuable time was not wasted searching and gathering the outlying hill land when perhaps only one horse was required.

The Normans crippled the economy totally by ensuring that anything which could not be of use to them was destroyed. This meant killing those animals they could not drive off, razing buildings to the ground, burning standing crops, and breaking tools and equipment. Rebuilding was difficult as labour was at a premium. As the Normans had concentrated their raids on the most densely inhabited centres, the only ponies they were able to take or put to the sword were the poorer quality riding or pack animals. Lack of time prevented them from gathering the high ground where the brood mares, youngstock and breeding stallions were kept so, in practical terms, only surplus stallions or work animals were taken. It also meant that there were no broken and trained horses left to help recultivate the land after the Norman troopers had departed.

Those villagers who escaped death at the hands of the Normans were left with no means of livelihood and many took refuge in the dense woodlands or on the high ground, fearing another wave of Norman raids. There they lived a pitiful hand-to-mouth existence based on hunting and foraging as their forebears had done. Their only livestock consisted of goats and ponies which grazed the moorland in summer and, with the absence of hay, could be wintered on browse – the leafs and branches of deciduous trees harvested in summer and dried.

Monks writing in the late eleventh century recorded with horror that refugees in the wilderness had been driven by starvation to eat horsemeat. The practice had been common in earlier times, associated with the pagan cults of Odin and Freya. Having been weaned off eating horseflesh by more enlightened missionary thinking, this reverting to old ways must have seemed like a rebirth of paganism. Curiously, the disdain for eating horsemeat has persisted in this country right up to the present day. Nevertheless, circumstances forced the issue and for several decades at least breeding ponies for meat, supported by goat herding, became the mainstay of the northern economy. As the poor quality ponies would have been eaten first, the effect was a clearout of inferior stock and an escalation in the selective breeding of ponies.

When re-colonisation of the old settlements began, the villagers had more ponies than cattle and were compelled to use them for all types of haulage work and on the land, as oxen were by then scarce.

The only farmsteads and arable lands left untouched by the Norman troopers were almost exclusively church property, as the raiders had implicit instructions not to molest monastic houses or their tenants as they purported to have taken no part in the uprisings. In many but not all cases the instructions were heeded, although some tenants in outlying areas suffered losses, if not from the Normans, from refugees of ransacked settlements who had found armed robbery an easier option than herding goats and ponies in the hills.

Many French abbeys set up new houses in the north of England, mainly Cistercians as the order had a reputation for sound agricultural management. Sheep were their speciality, as they had been in France, and were kept for their wool and also for their milk which was made into cheese. Sheep thrived on the rough grazing, making them ideal stock for the vast expanses of moorland found in the north of England but, for them to survive, the wolf population had to be eliminated. This was undertaken by the Abbots and Priors, their tenants, and even professional 'wolvers' who were employed for the purpose. This activity needed horses, and the local black ponies proved ideal, being strong and surefooted with tireless stamina for long hunts on the high moorlands.

Sheep husbandry also needed horsepower for the shepherds who had to ride long distances between the farms or 'granges' and the sheep pastures. Even more was needed after the annual shearing to transport the fleeces back from the clipping folds to the farms or monastries, where they were sorted before being taken to market or to the ports from whence north-country wool was exported.

The Cistercian monks of Furness Abbey, one of the largest monastic houses in the northwest, were among the first to use pack ponies in appreciable numbers in the Lake District. They used the ponies to carry the wool clip from their extensive sheep farms around Hawkshead to the abbey near Barrow in Furness. By the thirteenth century, there was already a brisk trade for wool to Belgium and France, and the enterprising monks supplied the raw materials for the cloth manufacturers across the Channel. Buyers from as far away as Italy were known to have visited the north of England in medieval times, sampling the wool and placing orders.

All over the north there is still evidence of the old packways – green tracks or 'trods' used by the pack trains. Shallow streams were forded but, where there was any danger of the water being deep enough to wet the load, special pack horse bridges were built. Several fine examples are still to be seen in parts of the Lake District, some dating back to the thirteenth century when the monks originally built them. The distinctive feature of these narrow bridges built entirely of dry stone is that the single track, just wide enough for one pony, had a wall on either side to prevent a pony slipping over should it stumble but low enough not to catch the load on either side of the pony.

An early pack horse bridge built by Cistercian monks around the thirteenth century. The bridge is at Pennington, near Ulverston, Cumbria, and is on the old pack horse route between Hawkshead and Furness Abbey.

Even in pre-Roman times, pack ponies were occasionally shod, especially if they were used on stone-flagged tracks or on rough tracks strewn with loose stones or gravel. In the Lake District the ponies were never shod, partly because nearly all the pack 'trods' were green tracks but more because the Fell ponies used had the characteristic hard resilient hoofs which are still a feature of the breed.

Such was the demand for horsepower to support the thriving new agriculture of the north that, at the end of the fourteenth century, five farms belonging to one of the north-country abbeys each kept on average twelve ponies. Most monastic houses bred their own mounts and evidently kept their brood mares on the marginal land, as in earlier times, as tenants sometimes paid part of their rents by service or 'boon work', which duties included rounding up the Abbot's mares and foals annually on the 'waste'.

Although mining had been going on in the north since before Roman times, the monks did much to promote the extraction of all types of minerals from the ground, chiefly lead-ore and a little coal and iron-ore. This needed to be transported from the mines to the coastal towns and ports where it could be smelted, and pack trains again proved to be the most feasible way of doing it.

The development of the Fell breed throughout the later Middle Ages and into Tudor times was barely perceivable. Being in a relatively isolated area, outside influencing factors which affected other developing breeds in other parts of the country rarely penetrated into Fell territory. There were no major towns or ports, no important roads, no busy traffic bringing foreign breeds of horses to interbreed with the local stock, unlike the New Forest pony, for example, whose breeding ground was cut by the busy highways between Winchester, Salisbury and Southampton. Consequently, the Fell pony had little scope for variation from the established stamp of conformation, colour and size and, perhaps with the exception of the Exmoor pony, no other native breed has remained so consistent in type for so long nor is as easy to recognise and identify.

Up until this point, once the Fell pony foundation stock had been established as a new breed, the only outside blood brought in comprised a small percentage of ponies of other regional breeds brought home to the north by returning Pictish raiding parties, a number of Irish ponies, and small but regular infiltrations of Galloway ponies from the southwest area of Scotland.

The stallion Heltondale Rambler II, bred by Mr W. S. Noble and owned by Mrs R. H. Ball. The Fell pony has remained consistent in type for hundreds of years.

The Irish ponies were introduced by Norsemen who had originally settled in Ireland and then gradually migrated to the north of England, as evidenced in Cumbria by place names like Ireby and Ireton. They brought with them a type of Irish pony known as a *kapall*, the name being a Norse corruption of the old Irish word, *capaill*, meaning a pony. As the Norse had a variety of words in their language for horse, it is almost certain that the reason for using the old Irish word was to describe a particular stamp of animal rather than horses in general. In the thirteenth century, the word was respelt *capul* and it was in common use not only in the north but in other parts of the country as well. Chaucer mentions *capuls* in his works. Not surprisingly, the name crops up frequently in place names in Cumbria, sometimes in its pure form as in Capelrigg, or more commonly distorted to chapel or castle as in Castlerigg near Keswick. Despite the fact that the Norse-Irish, like the Picts, were great stone carvers there is little evidence of what the Irish *capul* was like. Bearing in mind that Friesian horses were shipped to Ireland in Roman times and that an Irish breed of pony, now extinct, developed as a result, it is possible that the *capul* may have been similar to the Fell. This may have explained why, like the Galloway, it was so easily absorbed into the Fell pony breed without altering it in any noticeable way.

The Galloway pony was very much the Scottish counterpart of the Fell pony, being developed from an initial cross between local native mares and Friesian stallions. These tireless black ponies were noted for their inherent qualities of stamina and speed, and they were used in large numbers by the Scottish cattle drovers who regularly came down into northern England to trade Kyloe cattle at the famous fairs and sales held all over the Lake District. Other drovers took their cattle further afield to Manchester, Birmingham and London, using the old drovers' roads like the Gallowgate, a green road that wound its way through Cumbria with watering places and safe overnight stops, like Shap Thorn, at regular intervals. As these Scotsmen were great dealers and traders, the sale of Galloway ponies to the farmers and shepherds of the region was inevitable, and this quiet but regular trade in ponies continued right up until the nineteenth century when indiscriminate breeding caused the demise of what should have become the tenth British native breed.

Proof of the importance of Galloway ponies is indicated by writers like a certain Dr Anderson who, in the 1700s, wrote of these remarkable ponies that had been used to improve the Fell pony since pre-Tudor times. 'There was once a breed of small elegant horses in Scotland', he wrote, 'similar to those of Iceland and Sweden, and which were known by the name of Galloway.' His use of the past tense would suggest that the breed was in decline then, and it is significant that Samuel Johnson in his dictionary of 1755 mentions only the Galloway when assessing the equine stock of the north, describing it as 'a horse of not more than fourteen hands high, much used in the north'. Dr Anderson recorded that the best Galloways 'sometimes reached the height of fourteen hands and a half'. Sir Walter Gilbey in his book, *Thoroughbred and Other Ponies*, wrote of the Galloway: 'They played an active part in agricultural work in the lowlands of Scotland. In localities where no roads existed, and wheeled traffic was impossible, Galloways were used not only for riding but for the transport of agricultural produce.' He went on to add:

> Sledges were drawn by Galloways, which were also used to carry corn and general merchandise in pots and panniers. The purposes for which they were used indicated the desirability of increasing their height and strength, and with this end in view cross-breeding was commenced somewhere about the year eighteen hundred and continued for fifty years. The old Galloway after this period almost disappeared from all parts of the mainland, and survives only in such remote situations as the Island of Mull.

Again writing in the past tense about a breed close to extinction, Youatt wrote in 1851 that 'the Galloway was a horse of thirteen to fourteen hands in height once found in the South of Scotland on the shores of the Solway Firth; but now sadly degenerated through the attempts of the farmer to obtain a larger kind, better adapted for the purpose of agriculture'.

What percentage of Galloway blood went into the make-up of the present day Fell pony is difficult to estimate but its contribution must have been considerable. Even today, Cumbrian hill farmers of the older generation still refer to Fell ponies as Fell-Galloways, probably a vestige of past times when the two breeds were virtually indistinguishable in the north, and in other parts of the country the name Galloway is still occasionally used to describe a pony of around fourteen hands. In the last century a race for ponies under fourteen hands was held in Devon and advertised as a 'Galloway Race', such was the widespread fame and reputation of this amazing breed.

While the Galloway pony was sufficiently like the Fell in colour, type and size to be able to interbreed with it without altering its appearance, the great quality the Galloway passed on, before dying out itself, was its stamina. Ponies of the old border breed were renowned for their 'speed, stoutness, and surefootedness over a very rugged and mountainous country', as Youatt wrote in 1820. The ponies ridden by the

Scottish cattle drovers were expected to carry their owners on journeys of up to several hundred miles on meagre rations and sometimes to tight time schedules. A Galloway pony belonging to Dr Anderson carried him on his travels for twenty-five years, and during this time he twice rode the pony on a 150-mile journey, without stopping except for meal breaks which never lasted for longer than an hour. 'It came in at the last stage', wrote the doctor, 'with as much ease and alacrity as it travelled the first.'

Another exceptional feat was performed in 1701 at Carlisle, when a Galloway pony belonging to a man called Sinclair from Kirkby Lonsdale performed the extraordinary achievement of one thousand miles in one thousand hours, while fifty-three years later a pony of the same breed belonging to a sportsman named Mr Corker did one hundred miles a day for three consecutive days over the Newmarket course.

As the Galloway was an established breed by Norman times, its influence on the Fell pony was spread over many centuries, as raiding parties from over the border, cattle drovers, horse dealers, traders, gypsies and assorted other travellers brought ponies down into the north of England. In the thirteenth century, in the written records of Scottish raids on farms and settlements in the north, special mention is made of the men of Galloway who were distinguished from other semi-professional mounted thieves from over the border by the swiftness of the ponies they rode.

Although a series of royal decrees had been issued prior to Henry VIII's ascension to the throne with the aim of improving the quality and size of British horses, their effect had been very limited and none had exercised any influence at all on the pony population of the country. Most of the laws introduced by Edward II concerned the minimum values of horses for export and, over the years, subsequent kings extended or amended these laws as they saw fit. Henry VII in 1507 passed a law making it an offence to export horses from Ireland to any place except England.

It was not until Henry VIII turned his attention to the improvement of the horse stock of Britain that any serious consideration was given to the many and varied native pony breeds. He issued a series of laws concerning the breeding of horses on common grazing land, with the intention of producing troop horses suitable for the light-horse element of his armies. It was not, as is often assumed, for the breeding of chargers for armoured knights. Seeing no practical value in stallions of less than fifteen hands or mares of less than thirteen hands, and to ensure the breeding of animals of the desired height, he enacted a law whereby the local magistrates of certain shires were responsible for an annual Michaelmastide drive. Any stallions or mares below the minimum height of fifteen hands and thirteen hands respectively, or any foals not showing the potential of gaining the necessary height, were slaughtered. The immense administrative workload of such a law together with insufficient government officials made implementation difficult and, for the most part, the law was ineffective. Nevertheless, the destruction of Exmoor, Dartmoor, Welsh and Cornish ponies reduced the numbers of these breeds substantially.

Another of Henry VIII's laws stated:

> Forasmuch as the breed of good and strong horses is a great help and defence to the realm and a great comoditie to the inhabitants thereof, which is now much decayed by reason that little stoned horses and nags be suffered to pasture in forests, etc. and to cover mares feeding there, therefore for the encrease of stronger horses hereafter be it enacted that no commoner or commoners within any forest, chase, moore, marish, heth, common or wast grounde at any time after the 31st March 1543 shall have or put forth to pasture in any such ground etc. any stoned horse or horses being above the age of two yeare and not being of the altitude and height of fifteen handfulls.

Fortunately, these laws were not applicable to all areas and the northern counties of Cumbria, Northumberland and Durham were exempt. Even so, the Fell pony was still indirectly affected by the passing of these laws because they encouraged the cross-breeding of native ponies with stallions of fifteen hands or more with the objective of producing youngstock that would not only make the minimum height to avoid the royal cull but would also be more saleable. It is highly probable that the trend of cross-breeding for size which caused the eventual extinction of the Galloway pony was instigated by the laws of Henry VIII. The practice was not feasible everywhere, however, as, in the hills of northwest England which had been a stronghold for the Fell pony since early times, the upland slopes where the ponies were still traditionally kept would not support larger animals. In the vast and isolated region to the west of the Pennine watershed on the exposed moorland overlooking Ullswater, Derwentwater, Wast Water and the other lakes, the true Fell pony grazed and bred unaware of royal decrees.

There was another more far-reaching way in which Henry VIII influenced pony breeds in the north, especially the Fell and Dales ponies, which was totally unconnected with his horse-breeding statutes. It was during his reign that the dissolution of the monasteries, abbeys and large religious houses was enforced. Since being set up after the Norman invasion, the monasteries had increased in size and wealth very considerably, mainly as a result of their innovative and highly efficient method of sheep farming which enabled them to use the poor quality hill land to maximum benefit. As well as land around the monasteries themselves, most owned outlying farms or 'granges' in addition to large tracts of hill land, often several days' ride from the monasteries, and used for the summering of the sheep flocks. Not only sheep but cattle and horses were kept.

The Cistercian monks, a white-robed order, who had houses at Lanercost in the north of Cumbria, Shap Abbey and Furness Abbey, bred distinctive white cattle, the breed originating with the monks at Whalley Abbey in Lancashire and later to be officially recognised as British White cattle. They also kept and bred white horses, the colour serving as an easily recognisable mark of monastic ownership. Since horses had first been domesticated, white horses were believed to possess magical powers and they figured prominently in mythology and folklore. Despite the fact that the attribution of mystical qualities to white horses was pagan in origin, the adoption of both horses and cattle of this colour was widespread by monastic houses in the north.

It is highly likely that, unlike the white cattle which were developed into a breed, the white horses kept by the monks were not of any specific type and their colour was the only consistent trait they had in common. The majority of the abbeys bred their own horses according to their needs. These included *capuls* for packwork which would in most cases have been Fell ponies; palfreys for general riding, hunting and business; and cobs, or 'rouncies' as they were more commonly called at the time, which were ridden by the estate managers when visiting outlying farms or attending markets.

Up until the reformation, the most usual colour for the Fell pony was black with a few bays and browns and an occasional dun. Evidence of this comes from a document describing about 250 ponies, the bulk of which will have been of Fell breeding, requisitioned in the north of England during the sixteenth century for use in retaliations against the Scots, who were again coming over the border in raiding parties. With three exceptions (which were chestnut and which can be discounted as probably introduced into the area from elsewhere), all the listed animals complied with the established Fell colours of black, bay and brown. It is interesting to note that there were more mares and geldings respectively in the list than stallions, which would indicate that the parallel practices of gelding and selective breeding were gaining ground.

32

With the dissolution of the monasteries, lands were confiscated, buildings allowed to fall into disrepair, and stock sold off locally. After the reformation, the white horses were dispersed throughout the north and were absorbed into the Fell stock. As had been proved before, the Fell pony had inherited the prepotency of its Friesian ancestor which enabled it to withstand occasional introductions of foreign blood without losing its characteristic type. As such, the white horses had no long-term effect on the Fell's conformation, size or colour, and black continued to be the dominant colour. However, the grey element had now been introduced into the breed, and grey is a colour which comes and goes genetically in all breeds carrying the grey gene. Since the reformation, the occurrence of grey Fells has been recorded at regular intervals. As a grey horse or pony of any breed must have one grey parent to pass its colour on, it only needed a popular grey stallion covering mares in a

Grey Fell stallion in the 1980s: Mountain Dew of Cleveland, owned by Mr P. Lawson and ridden by his daughter, Sheena.

particular region to cause a spate of grey youngstock, and this fact has ensured the survival of grey as an official breed colour right up to the present day.

Throughout history the term 'horse' has been used in a general sense and without particular relevance to the size of animal. In decrying animals of less than thirteen hands, Henry VIII's laws still referred to them as horses, and in 1701 the Rev. John Bland described Shetland ponies as 'a sort of little horses called Shelties'. The word 'pony' is of Scottish origin and is generally attributed to one of two sources. The first is a possible derivative of the French word 'poulain', meaning foal, which is feasible as French was the second language of the Scottish upper classes. The second is derived from the Scottish word 'pow', meaning the poll, as the first recorded spelling of the word was 'powney', and the area around the poll including the ears is usually acknowledged to be an indication of pony character. Samuel Johnson in his dictionary written in 1755 concluded: 'I know not the original of this word, unless it be corrupted from puny.' John Byng, writing at the end of the eighteenth century, distinguished between Galloways and ponies, although other writers used the word 'pony' indiscriminately, making it impossible to draw any conclusions from the use of the word.

During the reign of Elizabeth I, skewbald as a colour was introduced into northern England and the Scottish borders by a new class of itinerant trader, known as a 'tinker' north of the border, and as a 'potter' on English soil. Despite a proliferation of these most shrewd of travelling salesmen throughout Stuart and into Hanoverian

times, their distinctive brown and white horses, later joined by piebalds, never posed more than a superficial threat to the purity of the Fell pony. Although there were coloured Fell ponies, as proved by some early entries in the stud books, the colour was bred out of the breed in subsequent generations and is never seen in present-day examples of the breed. The potters got their name from the pottery they sold, and they transported their fragile wares by pack pony. Great skill was needed to pack the cargo in such a way that breakages were kept to a minimum. Like their contemporaries, the gypsies, the potters favoured coloured horses as they represented a sort of trademark, not unlike the Cistercian monks with their white horses. As the fancy colour was originally confined to the great war horses which were bred only by noblemen or at royal studs, and the general public with brood mares did not have access to stallions at these studs, the potters had to use their cunning to obtain the services of these inaccessible stallions. They did so by slipping their mares into the royal parks or breeding 'closes' where these stallions ran after nightfall, and reclaiming them before dawn. The same method is believed to be used by some potters to this day to obtain the services of chosen stallions without having to pay a stud fee. The great war horse ancestry of the potter's horses, plus their station in life as pack ponies, would lead us to expect them to have been strongly built cobby animals of around fourteen to fifteen hands, which would correspond well to the size and type of horse still used by the travelling fraternity and to be seen in large numbers at north-country gatherings like Brough Hill Fair. While piebald and skewbald may no longer be Fell colours, the remaining small percentage of alien blood would not have been sufficient to have influenced other aspects of the breed, especially as both the potter's type of horse and the Fell pony conformed to the traditional stamp of pack pony.

The earliest record there is of any individual stallion having an impact on the breed concerns a famous stallion named Lingcropper, stories of whom, handed down by word of mouth, predate the first registered Fells by 150 years. The stallion in question was found on Stainmore, an area of bleak moorland in what used to be the county of Westmorland but is now part of Cumbria, cropping the ling heather from whence came his name. No one knew where he came from or how he got there because, although he was saddled and bridled, there was no rider anywhere in sight. It is probable that he had been used in border raids and skirmishes and, as after every battle there were always loose horses, had wandered to Stainmore where he was found. Popular legend claimed that he was connected with the uprising of 1745 although there was no evidence to substantiate this. It is also possible that he originated in Scotland and was a Galloway pony and not a Fell. Whatever he was is of less importance than the fact that he must have been a pony of some distinction for his name to crop up so regularly in ballads and stories popular at the time. Lingcropper was also a sire of great importance and his progeny were to carry his name forward for many generations. If for no other reason, this interesting tale contains the first reference to a named pony made legendary by popular acclaim.

The most famous and influential of early stallions was not foaled until the end of the nineteenth century, however, and he was a black pony with a white star called Blooming Heather. He was bred by a Mr Tunstall of Stainmore in 1880 and could very easily have been a descendant of Lingcropper. His importance lies in the fact that he appears in more Fell pony pedigrees than any other stallion. It was said that Teesdale was famous for three things: 'a bit of steel shipbuilding, High Force and Blooming Heather', while another commentator described him as 'possibly the most famous sire of Fell ponies that ever lived'. Blooming Heather's sire, Little John, was reputedly 'one of the fastest trotting ponies that was ever known in England' and he was never beaten in the showring although, at the time, this probably only extended to those shows in the immediate locality. Little John was eventually sold abroad for the then astronomical sum of £180. Many of Blooming Heather's progeny inherited their grandsire's trotting speed, and a bystander once saw one of Blooming Heather's sons trotting against the clock on the hard road with the owner's son at the other end of the rope and riding a big horse full gallop to keep up. At a time when £10 would buy a good broken pony, the sum of £200 was refused for a colt and filly by the famous stallion.

Roy B. Charlton, senior, of The Linnels, Hexham, could remember staying at the High Force Hotel in Teesdale with his parents in the 1890s when he was just a young boy. They were told they had just missed seeing the famous Fell pony stallion, Blooming Heather, as his owner, Mr Gibson, had set off for his home, Widdy Bank, somewhere on that wild moor only half an hour earlier. After dinner that evening, Roy started out for Widdy Bank which his map showed to be five miles up stream and away on the moors. It was dark when he got there and he rapped on the back door of the house. After a time it was opened by the old man with a hurricane lamp in his hand and, after his initial surprise at receiving a caller so young and so late at night, he took the boy to see the famous pony. Recalling the details of the visit as an elderly man himself, Roy wrote:

We went into a miserable old stable where the little horse was standing up to his

36

Blooming Heather, foaled 1880, owned by John Gibson, Middleton in Teesdale. This photograph, taken c. 1890, is believed to be the only one in existence of this famous stallion.

knees in a bracken bed. He was munching dreadful looking hay, and there were cocks and hens roosting all along the stall tops at the other end of the stable. Blooming Heather and his surroundings disappointed me dreadfully. He was a common looking pony, with not a neat head, but he appeared to be standing on good sound legs and feet. I only saw him by the light of the dirty old oil lamp, but I can remember him perfectly, and I am writing of just fifty years ago.

Whatever he was like, Blooming Heather undoubtedly had more influence on the breed than any other single pony.

Up until the late nineteenth century, the name 'Galloway' was used generically to refer not only to genuine ponies of the old Scottish breed but also to Fell ponies or indeed any other type of pony of around fourteen hands. For a time, Fell ponies were referred to as Brough Hill ponies, after the famous horse fair where so many of these ponies changed hands, and then, in 1898, the National Pony Society officially named the breed 'Fell'. As the other native breeds took their names from their home area, as in Dartmoor, Exmoor or New Forest, the Fell would probably have followed suit had its home area not spread over more than one county. Accordingly, they named it after the type of terrain it lived on and they used the old Norse word 'fell', meaning a hill or stretch of moorland. The name was accepted in the north and has remained the same ever since.

4 The uses of the Fell pony over the centuries

From Tudor times up until the late eighteenth century, the political upheavals, Civil War, disasters and triumphs that affected the rest of the country never penetrated into the home territory of the Fell pony. Since the reformation, the agriculture of the north had fallen into the hands of men who were little more than smallholders. Many combined their modest farming activities at home with paid part-time employment for larger farmers known in the north as yeomen. Most of these small farmers kept a Fell pony out of necessity. It was needed to pull a light plough or harrows, pony-sized versions of which still turn up with regularity at farm sales in the Lake District. It was required to help with haymaking or harvest, carry the farmer when he shepherded his flocks on the high ground, and take him and his family to church or market in a trap occasionally. In addition, mares were expected to rear a foal every year which could be sold as a cash crop in the autumn to supplement the meagre income of the farmer. It was quite usual for a brood mare to work all day in the fields while her foal was left shut up in a building at home, the mare being brought in to allow her foal to suck mid morning and afternoon when the men enjoyed a brief break. Foals soon learnt the art of getting their head under the cart shaft to get a drink. A retired farmer from Coniston told me of a Fell pony used on a farm in the district when he was a young man which carted the hay in from the fields every year for thirty years without a break, and he himself remembered ploughing with a Fell pony and a Clydesdale horse side by side. Isolated from the outside world, the Fell pony probably would have continued thus indefinitely had the Industrial Revolution not come along to give it a role of vital importance in the economic expansion of the north.

The mineral wealth of the north of England had first been exploited in Roman times and had continued, spasmodically and on a small scale, ever since. Parts of the northwest were rich in iron-ore and lead-ore for which there was an increasing demand during the Middle Ages and later times. Once excavated, the ore had to be transported from the mines across country to the smelting works on the northeast coast, and this operation was made difficult by the hilly moorland terrain and the lack of roads, canals or navigational rivers. Those roads built by the Romans had quickly fallen into disrepair and, with no roads suitable for wheeled vehicles, the use of carts was considerably restricted. Those that were in use tended to be heavy and clumsy and needed regular repair, especially to the wheels and axles which wore out quickly. Generally, they were only used in the summer as in winter the wheels sank into the wet ground, even when the cart was unladen, making it inoperable. More common throughout the north was the sled, a horsedrawn wooden platform on runners which was better suited to the hilly ground and much used for transporting hay and harvested crops in from the fields. Like the cart, the use of the sled was restricted to fairly smooth ground, so it could only be used either in the fields or on the upper slopes or fells where bracken was harvested and dried to be used for bedding stock in winter. As the mined ore was both heavy and bulky, the use of carts or sleds to transport it long distances was out of the question.

The pack-horse system for transporting goods had been well established throughout the country for many hundreds of years when the exploitation of the mineral wealth and labour force of Britain, posthumously known as the Industrial Revolution, got under way in the late eighteenth century. The Fell pony, which had been created as a pack and haulage breed originally, was suddenly in demand in very large numbers, as it fulfilled exactly the requirements of the 'lademen' or professional packmen. The lademan was not named because he led the ponies, as is sometimes thought, for they were neither led nor driven but worked loose headed, following the lead of a bell-horse which was either led or ridden. The use of the bell-horse, named for the bell worn around its neck, as leader was very much tied in with the ponies' herd instinct, and is not dissimilar to the use of a sheep with a bell, known as the 'bell-wether' since Chaucer's time, to head the flocks grazing on common

Fell pack ponies carrying wool sacks. A reconstruction of the system used in the nineteenth century when, at one time, it was estimated that 300 Fell ponies left Kendal each working day carrying wool, produce and manufactured goods.

ground. There were basically two types of lademan: those who worked in a very localised area, transporting the farmer's corn to the village mill where it was ground for domestic use, or collecting the wool clip from outlying farms for merchants; and those who made regular scheduled journeys between the bigger towns or ports with 'trains' of up to twenty animals. It was the latter who were responsible for carrying the lead-ore and iron-ore to the coastal smelting works. The lademen were highly skilled, as the job of loading each individual animal was an art in itself. Not only had the load to be secured so that it did not slip off, but the weight of the load had to be distributed evenly on either side of the pony's spine. An imbalanced load could have worked loose causing back injuries or even falling off altogether.

The staffing ratio for pack-horse trains varied according to the type and weight of load and the distance being covered. On local journeys, one man might be responsible for ten or more ponies, whereas on long hauls the staffing ratio was more usually one man to every four ponies. As the standard load or 'seam' was two hundredweight (100kg) per pony, most carriers transporting ore worked gangs of ten ponies carrying a ton between them. This usually meant employing two men and a boy to work with each gang, as all three were needed for the standard loading and unloading procedure necessary on long journeys with overnight stops. To unload, the two men had to be able to lift the packsaddle complete with its sixteen stone cargo while the boy, who had undone the girth, led the pony out from under. The packsaddle was then lowered to the ground by the two men. To reload next morning, the boy held the pony in front of the packsaddle which the two men then lifted on from behind and held steady until the boy fastened and tightened the girth. If pack animals much larger than a Fell pony had been used, the men would have been unable to lift the packsaddle on and off by this system.

The ore was carried in two large wicker panniers attached, one either side, to a wooden packsaddle. Some packsaddles had integral padding, although most simply rested on a thick blanket laid across the pony's back, and the load was secured in place with a thick girth sometimes assisted by a breeching strap that went around the pony's hindquarters to prevent the packsaddle from slipping forward.

The system for unloading the ore from the panniers at the smelting works also required great skill. The pony was held by the boy while one of the men crouched down behind it and withdrew the long iron pins that fastened the hinged flat bases of the panniers, allowing the ore to be released into a small pile on either side of the pony. It was imperative that both pins were pulled simultaneously or the uneven weight in the panniers would have caused the packsaddle to slip to one side.

Most of the lademen were private operators working on regular contract for the mines or smelters, although in later times the droves of pack animals were often owned by the mines and smelting works themselves.

The trains of Fell ponies supplying the smelters with their essential raw material provided a service that was reliable, inexpensive and fast. They covered up to 240 miles a week, working seven days a week, and many ponies carried ore in this fashion for year after year without a break. Although they were never shod, lameness was very rare and hereditary unsoundness unknown. The ponies always travelled at a walk but the active, long-reaching stride of the Fell pony meant they were able to cover in excess of thirty miles a day quite easily. John Byng, later to become Viscount Torrington, rode around Britain in 1792 and kept a detailed diary of his travels, in which he mentions trains of pack ponies coming down from the lead mines in Swaledale. Forty years later, William Cobbett, another early traveller and writer, wrote from North Shields on the east coast where many of the smelting works were situated of ponies being used to draw small two-wheeled carts filled with lead-ore. We can assume that these carts were only used for moving the ore at the works as pack ponies were in common use until the arrival of the railways. Significantly, Cobbett also mentions in his diary at the same time that a railway was in construction between Carlisle and Newcastle.

The cost of haulage by pack pony varied little throughout the area and was kept down by the low overheads of the operators. The ponies were inexpensive to buy and could be expected to work for many years on meagre rations. Supplementary feeding was rare, except in winter, and most existed on whatever poor-quality grazing was available at the stopping places. Around 1770, the cost of a load from Backbarrow, near Ulverston to Coniston, a distance of about twenty-two miles, was eight pence for a two hundredweight load. From Coniston to Eskdale cost a shilling a load, although there were discounts for long distances and regular contracts. As well as iron and lead-ore, coal, slate and lime, an essential ingredient in the smelting process, were also transported by pack pony.

Many interesting and entertaining stories, many of them in the form of north-country ballads, were told about the pack trains and the lademen. One tale in particular concerned a string of Fell ponies which operated on the pack route between Kendal and Whitehaven. The drove was led by an old black stallion who had been used as a bell-horse for many years. He knew his job inside out and set the pace for the rest to follow in the customary manner. The overseer, who was mounted on another pony, had a great fondness for alcohol, and he used to ride ahead of the drove to the first inn and stay there until the drove had passed. A little later he would ride on to the next inn, passing the drove in between, and he kept this up all the way to Whitehaven and back.

The work of the pack ponies was not restricted to mineral cargoes solely, and there are monastic records of whole porpoises, to be eaten by the monks on special fast days, being carried on the backs of the local ponies. In her book *Through England on a side saddle*, the nineteenth-century author Celia Fiennes mentions the pack ponies used by the people of Kendal. She wrote: 'They use horses on which they have a sort of pannyers, some close, some open, but they strewn full of hay, turff and lime and dung and everything they would use.'

The expansion of the industrial towns in Lancashire and further afield brought an ever-increasing demand for farm produce which the merchants of the market town of Kendal supplied by sending meat, butter, cheese and other perishable goods by pack train. It is recorded that around 1825, twenty Fell ponies laden with produce left Kendal each week for London, another eighteen made the weekly journey to Wigton, and a further twenty travelled to Whitehaven. Two droves of fifteen ponies each travelled between Kendal and Penrith each week. So reliable were the pack trains that merchants in London, Manchester and other major cities were able to offer their customers fresh Lakeland produce all year round. It was estimated at one time that over 300 Fell ponies left Kendal every working morning for destinations all over the country, carrying cargo as diverse as woollen stockings, tanned hides, live chickens, fresh fish and bolts of cloth.

In very remote areas of the Lake District, it was quite usual, when someone died, to transport the corpse wrapped in a sheet or in a crudely made coffin by pack pony across country to the nearest church for burial. At least one of the old pack horse trods often used for this purpose is known as the corpse road. A much-told story dating back to the last century is related of the Fell pony mare being led over the corpse road with the coffin of the deceased strapped to the packsaddle and accompanied by a group of mourners walking behind. Somehow the mare got loose and, to the astonishment of the mourners, galloped off back to the fell from whence she came with the coffin intact. Attempts to recapture her failed and it was not until six weeks later that the mare was finally caught and the dead man committed to the grave to the great relief of his relatives.

Cumbrian smugglers who were very active during the seventeenth and eighteenth centuries also used Fell ponies to carry contraband when English taxation laws encouraged an illicit trade in spirits, tobacco and salt. The goods were generally imported from the Isle of Man and hidden in or around the Cumbrian ports like Whitehaven, ready for secret shipment to Carlisle, Penrith or Kendal. The smugglers who plied this trade, under threat of being dealt with severely by the authorities if caught, transported the contraband at night, using remote hill passes and tracks and with the ponies' hoofs bound with sacking to muffle any sound likely to draw unwanted attention. Some smugglers like the famous Lanty Rigg evaded the customs officials for years and became folk heroes in the locality.

A few Fells were employed for surface work at the mines and, when horizontal shafts as opposed to vertical sunken shafts were introduced which were large enough to admit a Fell pony, some were also used underground, although generally Shetland or Shetland crosses predominated. One coal mine in Northumberland used Fell ponies for both underground and surface work until well into this century.

The value of the Fell pony for speedy and efficient cross-country transport was soon recognised by the Post Office, which used considerable numbers of ponies for deliveries from their branches especially in more remote areas of the Lake District. Although mail coaches were in general use in the northwest of England after 1785, mounted post boys were employed for deliveries in many regions long after this date and the majority were mounted on Fell ponies. Where the roads were bad, and more particularly in winter, a Fell pony was often the only feasible means of transporting the mail to isolated villages or hill farms. Occasionally, the pony was put to a Royal Mail trap, which was a light two-wheeled vehicle with a double seat for the postman and an enclosed boot just large enough to accommodate a bag of mail. One Fell stallion, Old Lingcropper, who was a direct descendant of his namesake of Stainmore fame, carried the mail between Keswick and Penrith, a distance of eighteen miles, for twelve years every day without a break. One of Old Lingcropper's descendants was also employed by the Post Office and drew a Royal Mail trap. In bad weather and more especially in winter when deep snow hampered deliveries, a second pony was harnessed up and the two Fells were driven in tandem. When its Fell ponies were not being used in an official capacity, or at quiet times, one Post Office branch offered its ponies for public hire and hung a notice in its window to this effect.

From early Victorian times tourists began visiting the Lake District and all the larger hotels offered stabling facilities as well as horses and vehicles for hire. One or two of the hotels and livery stables advertised ponies for hire, forerunners of the many riding and trekking stables that would proliferate in the Lake District in later times. Lady E. M. Ascroft who, as a child with her sister, visited the Ambleside area in 1886 recalled hiring two Fell ponies from the Prince of Wales Hotel at Grasmere to ride up Helvellyn. As part of the modest hiring charge the hotel provided a male groom who led the pony all the way to the top of Helvellyn and back; their route went from Bridge House in Grasmere up the path by Tongue Ghyll to Grisedale Tarn and they returned home down Dunmail Raise. There were a number of Fells in the hotel's stable and Lady Ascroft remembered them as all being brown and rather small but extremely surefooted and agile over the roughest ground.

Even though the Fell was essentially a utility animal employed in both agriculture and industry, it also played a role in the sport and leisure activities of the region. The Vikings had introduced the sport of stallion fighting into Britain, although its popularity was short-lived and it was discontinued as Christianity became more widespread. The Church felt unable to condone the sport because of its connections with pagan fertility cults, as the stallions could only be induced to fight by the presence of an in-season mare. It was quickly replaced by racing, the Norse word for which was *hestaskeith*, and there is ample evidence of the popularity of the new sport in Cumbrian place names like High and Low Hesket and Hesket New Market. The word is derived from the old Norse verb, *skeitha*, meaning to pace or move both legs on one side simultaneously. In Britain, the Scandinavian sport was translated into ridden trotting races and by the nineteenth century trotting ranked alongside cock-fighting and Cumberland wrestling as one of the principal sports of the north country.

Many of the trotting matches of later times were run in conjunction with the shepherds' meets, held every year at the end of the summer partly for the purpose of claiming lost sheep and, more importantly, as annual social gatherings. The ponies were raced between stone markers laid out for the purpose, and were always ridden bareback and with just a simple bridle or rope halter. The stone markers used for trotting races can still be seen on High Street, the old Roman green road which crosses the fells near Bampton. Traditionally, the riders were served bread and ale before they raced, and the winner received a barrel of beer as his prize. At the smaller races the winner's prize was more likely to be a jug of ale to be consumed there and then, or a small purse of money. Other trotting races were the result of wagers made between the Cumbrian shepherds with their Fell ponies and Scottish cattle drovers passing through the region with their Kyloe cattle and Galloway ponies. The latter were more likely to be run on the hard road over a measured mile course, like the one at Orton, near Penrith, which started at the gates of Petty Hall in the middle of the village and finished at Street Farm exactly one mile away. At Tebay, a grassy stretch still known as the Fair Mile was another well-known venue. Heavy bets were placed on the races and fast ponies became famous locally.

Mr Jim Bell attired in traditional dress and riding Waverhead Magic in a reconstruction of the Fell pony trotting races which were once so popular in the Lake District in the nineteenth century.

Fells were used so extensively for trotting that several strains were developed within the breed specifically for this purpose. Most notable were the ponies bred by the Dargue family of Bow Hall, Dufton, near Appleby in Westmorland. The strain, which was founded early in the nineteenth century, was selectively bred to produce ponies which were fast trotters, and some of the characteristic bone and substance of the breed was sacrificed in the process. Dargue ponies were lighter in bone than the typical Fell, and a great many of them were grey. However, none of the stamina and hardiness was lost and the performance of these ponies, the descendants of which are still owned and bred by the Dargue family today, speaks for itself. Strawberry Girl, a 13.2 hh grey mare bred by the Dargues, won many trotting races and handicaps including the Borough Stakes at Blackpool on 17 July 1882, the first prize for which was a purse of £60. She also enjoyed innumerable wins and placings under saddle and in harness in the showring, and she won the class for the best harness pony under 13.2 hh at Bootle and Farnsworth shows. A copy of *The Field* in 1866 carried an advertisement for one of the Dargues' trotting ponies:

> Dark grey pony. Five years. Thirteen two hands high. Trots one mile in three minutes carrying twelve stones. Goes well in harness. The property of J. Dargue, Bow Hall.

So acclaimed did the Dargues' ponies become that in the early 1920s, they were selling ponies to Boardale Pit for £60–70, which was a very high price in those days.

Other ponies of the Dargues' breeding found employment in other fields of activity. Just before the 1914 war a butcher in Dufton bought a brown pony from them which was ridden to hounds regularly. Its performances in the hunting field often put seasoned hunters to shame and it was an accomplished jumper over the most difficult country. This used to annoy a certain J. Rigg of Appleby, who was always well mounted, so much that when war broke out and Mr Rigg was appointed as a remount officer he got his revenge by commandeering the pony, even though it was under the minimum height required.

Other famous trotting Fells included Jack's Delight, a stallion bred by the Relphs of Southernby, which at one time was advertised to trot 'any Galloway in the world'. In those days before motorised horse transport, the world usually meant within the counties of Cumberland and Westmorland. In the case of Jack's Delight, breeding for speed at the trot had not been to the detriment of conformation or action as he was also shown four times and won every time out.

47

The Charlton family of Hexham also bred many fast trotting Fells including Little Jean, a dark brown mare of only 12.1 hh, who, unlike the Dargues' ponies, was a heavily built, old-fashioned type of pony but very active. She made light work of trotting a mile in three minutes carrying a ten-stone (64 kg) rider, and she became so famous that on one occasion when she was driven from Hexham to Brough Hill horse fair a huge crowd turned out to witness her arrival.

The performances of these Fell ponies eventually came to the ears of Tom Jones Evans of Craven Arms in Shropshire, a great Welsh pony breeder and enthusiast. His father owned an outstanding Welsh Cob stallion called Comet, foaled in 1851, and described as 'a heavy cob standing nearly fifteen hands in height'. Old Evans sent Comet up into Westmorland to compete against the local trotting Fells, and at the end of the season he left him at Orton in the care of an elderly farmer named Bell. As the Welshman was leaving Bell's farm, he gave the owner's son a sovereign, a huge sum in those days, and said: 'Now, my lad, I am leaving in your care the greatest trotting cob that ever came out of Wales. Take care of him.' The following spring, Evans returned to Orton and was delighted to find Comet in splendid condition. After a few practice runs and some extra feeding they matched him against time on the main Shap turnpike, a stretch of hard road which runs from the tollbar just south of the village to the top of Shap fell and back, a very hard course. As a very old man the recipient of the sovereign could still recall that day, and remembered that Comet trotted ten miles in thirty-two minutes carrying a twelve-stone man. It was an outstanding feat for an untrained cob, but Comet was outstanding, and he went on to make a reputation for himself in the north as a performer without equal. It was said that people travelled miles to see the great horse trot, not least of all the gypsies and travelling people who frequented the horse fairs and were knowledgeable judges of 'a good goer'. On one occasion when Comet was being raced through Shap village and the local people had turned out to watch, a child ran across the road as Comet was approaching at great speed. The child tripped and fell, but the cob stepped over him in his stride, and the child was picked up unharmed. Although Evans could never be persuaded to sell his cob, Comet remained in Westmorland for the rest of his days and sired many very good ponies. The story is of particular interest as some of Comet's descendants were absorbed into, and reputedly did much to improve, the Fell pony. Breeders believed that animals with Comet blood inherited his tremendous energy, soundness of constitution and stamina.

The appearance of Standardbred trotting horses around the turn of the century from Manchester and Glasgow, which were considerably faster than the Fells, caused the demise of pony trotting in the north, although in recent years traditional bareback 'trots' for Fell ponies have become a popular and entertaining innovation at one or two shows again.

In the late nineteenth century, the arrival of the railways, the internal combustion engine, and steam power on the land heralded the beginning of a serious decline in numbers for the breed. Suddenly outdated by more modern forms of power, many ponies were sold abroad for slaughter. Horsedrawn farm implements were discarded or converted to be drawn by tractors, traps were broken up and the wheel spokes used for ladder rungs, and harness was thrown out or burned.

In the towns and cities, street traders who were one-man operators still often preferred a pony and cart as it was far less expensive to buy and maintain than a van or small wagon, and for deliveries door to door it could also be more time effective. Fells were a favourite breed for this line of work as they were strong and docile and inexpensive to keep.

There were some jobs for which motorised power was unsuitable, and in its native

Mr W. S. Noble, owner of the Heltondale herd, out shepherding on a Fell pony in the 1950s.

hills the Fell pony continued to be used by hill farmers for all types of agricultural work and shepherding. With its inherent intuitive power, the Fell was a safe mount for riding on the moors when shepherding, as it would sense boggy and unsafe ground which needed to be avoided. Whether on hillsides with loose shaley top soil, on rocky tracks or in deep snow, the Fell could be relied upon to cope admirably. In recent years, the introduction of light cross-country motorbikes or more substantial three or four wheeled versions has reduced the number of Fell ponies still used for shepherding to a mere handful, although purists often believe a pony is still preferable as a motorbike can unsettle the sheep.

A few ponies were also used in the woods for snigging timber in areas inaccessible to a tractor, while others were used as shooting ponies on large estates or for bringing the grouse panniers down from the moors after a shoot. Fells are still occasionally used for this job on the royal estate at Balmoral. Roy B. Charlton sold many Fells from his famous Linnels stud as shooting ponies and, in the early part of this century, one of his customers kept thirty-two Linnel-bred Fell ponies at his shooting lodge in Ross-shire. On shooting days, all thirty-two were used by the members of the large parties who came for the sport. Other shooting ponies were sold from the Linnels to such prestigious customers as the fifth Earl of Lonsdale, who took a great interest in the breed and bred a number of good ponies himself.

While these occupations employed some Fells, demand for the breed slumped alarmingly in the first half of the twentieth century and it was not until the 1950s that the revival of horse riding and driving as a leisure activity saw an upturn in the breed's fortunes. Riding schools and trekking centres sprang up all over the country and especially in areas like the Lake District, where tourism was expanding rapidly. Proprietors of these establishments needed ponies which were docile and good natured so that they could be safely handled by inexperienced riders. They needed to be strong enough to carry an adult yet not too big for a child to manage, and they had to have the stamina and soundness to work all season. Ponies that were inexpensive to buy and economical feeders were secondary but important considerations. These requirements were very similar to those of the professional lademan of upwards of a hundred years earlier when he was selecting pack ponies, and the Fell proved as suited to carrying holiday riders as its predecessors were to carrying lead-ore. Not only did many of the trekking centres in the Lake District use Fells, but the old pack horse routes were re-discovered as ideal riding tracks away from the traffic and tourist busy spots and through some of the most beautiful country in the northwest.

Fells have been used for hunting since the days when a Lakeland hill farmer might

Ponies suitable for trekking. The late Miss Peggy Crossland, secretary of the Fell Pony Society for twenty-five years, leading one of the Society's rides.

have occasionally sneaked a day's sport with one of the local packs and riding the farm pony. Since then, examples of the breed have been ridden to hounds in many parts of the country and, providing the country is not too fast, they perform admirably. They excel in difficult going and are competent jumpers. Some years ago,

51

Mr Norman Laing riding the stallion, Twislehope Druid, out hunting with the Liddesdale Foxhounds in 1973.

the joint master of the Liddesdale foxhounds in the Scottish borders hunted hounds from a Fell pony for a number of seasons, and several members of his family as well as other hunt followers were similarly mounted. The master of the Haydon Foxhounds in Northumberland once borrowed a Fell from the Linnels stud back in the 1940s for an early morning cub hunt on Mr Charlton's land. An old fox was raised which gave them a wonderful day's sport over some rough country including some quite stiff jumping. So impressed was the pony's rider that he bought the animal and rode it home that evening.

In 1956 the British Driving Society was formed and, all over the country, lectures, demonstrations and rallies were organised in response to the overwhelming interest in harnessing horsepower once again. The driving revival offered the Fell pony another opportunity to show its versatility as the old skills of breaking and putting to were learned by a new generation of enthusiasts. Back in 1944, HRH Princess Margaret had won the private driving class at the Royal Windsor show driving a Fell mare, Windsor Gipsy, and the following year HM The Queen, then HRH Princess Elizabeth, repeated the win again with the same Fell pony driven to a phaeton. These early driving successes created a lot of interest in driving Fell ponies and encouraged other people to put their ponies between shafts. When combined driving, a new sport based on the ridden three-day event with dressage, cross country and obstacle driving phases, was introduced into this country in the early 1970s, the adaptable

Mrs J. Jenner driving Dalemain Columbine, a prolific winner in hand, under saddle, and in harness in the 1950s.

Miss M. Laing riding her homebred gelding, Twislehope Rex, in a hunter trial.

Fells were soon involved. Today, examples of the breed compete with success in all types of competitive driving.

The Riding for the Disabled movement, which includes driving in some of its groups, has used Fells for a number of years as they provide steady and safe mounts for quite severely disabled riders. One pony, Dalemain Dandelion, used in the 1980s by the Drum Riding Centre for the Disabled, near Edinburgh, won the Scottish final for the best pony for use by the Riding for the Disabled Association.

Excluding those ponies working in a recreational activity like trekking, very few

(Opposite page)

HRH The Duke of Edinburgh driving HM The Queen's team of Fell ponies at a combined driving event, *(above)* in the dressage phase and *(below)* through one of the hazards.

Fells are employed in a serious commercial capacity at the present time. The majority are privately owned and used for hacking, driving and competitive riding. Today there are more competitive opportunities for mountain and moorland ponies of all breeds than ever before, and Fells are regularly shown in-hand and under saddle, in harness, in working hunter classes, dressage, show jumping, hunter trials, long distance rides and in gymkhana classes.

The future for any breed of livestock, be it ponies, sheep, cattle or anything else, lies in that individual breed's ability to adapt to changing demands. The Fell, which was really developed as a draught and pack breed, has changed over the centuries to a riding pony primarily and ensured its survival in the process. There are very few equestrian activities for which the Fell is not suited, and its versatility helps to make it an ideal all-purpose ride and drive pony.

5 The influence of the Fell pony on other breeds

The National Pony Society was founded on 23 June 1893 'for the improvement and encouragement of the breeding of high class riding and polo ponies'. In fact, at that time, it was called the Riding and Polo Pony Society. Its foundation came about because, as the nineteenth century was drawing to a close, it became apparent that there was a great dearth of ponies of riding type. There was not a shortage of ponies but most, to meet the demands of the time, were predominantly harness types.

The War Office had learned from its experiences during the Boer War that the standard type of charger ridden by the regular cavalry was far from ideal when faced with the stresses of active military service. However, the few native ponies involved in the campaign had acquitted themselves with credit, and this had not gone unnoticed. Parliamentary commissions sat to discuss the weaknesses of the present remount system and to determine how suitable troop horses could be made available to the War Office. It was agreed that a percentage of native pony blood was highly desirable in a troop horse and, ultimately, premiums were offered in pony breeding areas for both mares and stallions of a type likely to produce animals suitable for mounted infantry. The offering of these premiums ran parallel to the aims of the Riding and Polo Pony Society who were trying to encourage pony breeders to revert to a riding type.

The introduction of polo from India in the 1870s furthered their cause, for cavalry officers found that those ponies fulfilling the polo requirements of weight-carrying capacity, size, speed and agility tended to have the conformation of a driving horse including harness action. They soon discovered, however, that a native pony mare of correct type put to a small Thoroughbred produced the ideal stamp of polo pony, and a new interest was taken in the mountain and moorland breeds.

In 1893, there were breed societies for only the Welsh, New Forest and Shetland ponies, and the Riding and Polo Pony Society's first priority was to coordinate the activities of these societies and to encourage the formation of breed societies for the other breeds. Five years later the Riding and Polo Pony Society opened sections in its stud books for the nine native breeds, and they elected a committee of four members in the north to inspect Fell ponies prior to registration to ensure that they were of true Fell pony type. The committee consisted of Mr W. W. Wingate-Saul, Lancaster; Mr R. W. Gibson, Orton; Mr W. Graham, Kirkby Thore; and Mr R. M. Malloch, Kirkby Stephen.

Mr Wingate-Saul was asked to write the first official breed description, and he summed up the characteristics of the Fell pony thus:

> A very powerful and compact cobby build, the majority having a strong middle piece with deep chest and strong loin characteristics, which, combined with deep sloping shoulders and fine withers, make them essentially weight carrying riding ponies. The prevailing – indeed the only colours are black, brown, bay and quite occasionally grey. I do not remember ever having seen a chesnut, and if I found one I should think it due to the introduction of other blood. The four colours prevail in the order named, the best animals often being jet black and usually without white markings unless it be a small white star. The head is pony-like and intelligent, with large bright eyes and well placed ears. The neck in the best examples being long enough to give a good rein to the rider. The hindquarters are square and strong with a well set on tail. The legs have more bone than those of any of our indigenous breeds, ponies under fourteen hands often measuring 8½ inches below the knee. Their muscularity of arm, thigh and second thigh is marvellous.
>
> Their habitat (having been bred for centuries on the cold inhospitable fells where they are still to be found) has caused a wonderful growth of hair, the winter coat being heavy and legs growing a good deal of fine hair, all of which, excepting some at the point of the heel, being cast in summer. Constitutionally they are hard as iron, with good all round action, and are very fast and enduring.

The system of having a northern committee, responsible to the National Pony Society as it was later to be known, was only partially effective. The farmers of Cumberland and Westmorland, who were the main breeders of Fell ponies, were reluctant to acknowledge the benefits of registering their ponies, especially as the society maintaining the records was at the other end of the country. They questioned the right and knowledge of the committee to pass or fail ponies for registration, many of the farming families having bred Fell ponies for generations, and being thrifty with their money they were not too keen to part with the registration fees.

Although the committee used Mr Wingate-Saul's breed description as a guideline, it was little more than a standard of excellence and failed to cover such important aspects of the breed as maximum height. The first Fell ponies were registered in Volume V of the Riding and Polo Pony Society's stud book, published in 1898, and to avoid possible confusion the words 'Brough Hill ponies' were included in brackets

after their section title. The registered ponies comprised two stallions, a bay and a brown, both 13.2 hh, by Blooming Heather and bred by Mr Gibson of Widdy Bank, and six mares. The latter all conformed to standard colours; four blacks, a bay and a brown, although one of the ponies had three white socks. However, they ranged in height from 12 hands to 14.1½ hh. The following year the committee inspected and passed as being of correct Fell type a piebald pony called The Mikado. Their indiscretion was due to the fact that they had met at The George Hotel in Penrith first and were quite drunk when they inspected the stallion. To camouflage their misdemeanor, they described the pony as black-brown with tan and white hind heels on the registration recommendation sent to the National Pony Society. In support of the registration, they also sent a detailed pedigree for the pony, included in Volume VI of the stud book, which recorded such illustrious ancestors of the pony as Old Grey Shales, Marshland Shales and Sportsman, who were Norfolk Trotters, and Flying Childers who was a son of the Darley Arabian. Not only was The Mikado a mile in under three minutes trotter, his dam, Dolly Varden, won both in the showring and in trotting matches. Her dam could trot four miles in 11 minutes 29 seconds, and won seventeen trotting races in succession and was only ever beaten once. She was killed in her thirty-sixth year.

Mrs J. H. Hutchinson's stallion, Tarnmoor Prince, twice champion at the Fell Pony Society stallion show.

The importance attributed to trotting ability was apparent in the early registrations, for in the lists of local show successes appended to some of the ponies' details trotting races often figured. One such pony was Trip, a brown mare bred by John Wearmouth of Brough in 1887, whose in-hand wins were matched by her successes in trotting races at Middleton in Teesdale, Stanhope, Brough and Warcop. The Riding and Polo Pony Society at this time began awarding silver medals and special prizes for Fell ponies at selected Lake District shows, and these were keenly contested, although in those days before motorised horse transport the entrants at any show would only come from within walking distance of the showground.

The Mikado was not the only aberration in the early days of Fell pony registrations and, despite definite rules on what was and was not to be allowed, other examples in the Fell register include a skewbald mare called Voreda who had been purchased at Brough Hill Fair and who won the Riding and Polo Pony Society medal at Penrith Show. There are other piebalds, a quarter-bred Arab, an entire out of a purebred Exmoor mare, and a black stallion whose ancestry included both Dales and Highland pony blood. The fifth Earl of Lonsdale, popularly known as the Yellow Earl because of his passion for the colour, owned a number of chestnut Fells, several having excessive white markings, and the Winder family of Caldbeck had a famous strain of roan ponies. As late as the 1950s, they were still breeding both blue and red roan ponies. The Teasdale family of Longlands bred a number of dun ponies but they invariably proved intractable and the last dun was sold to a blacksmith at Dalston in 1937.

Records kept for the year 1912 are of particular interest as they indicate the most common Fell colours at the time. That year, six premium-winning Fell stallions covered a total of 217 mares between them, an average of 36 each. Brown was the most common colour representing 59 mares, followed by 55 bays, 52 blacks, 30 greys, 13 chestnuts, 5 piebalds and, lastly, one roan, one dun, and one cream.

The inconsistencies in the colours of registered ponies was partly due to disagreement between pony breeders as to what was and was not acceptable as a typical Fell pony, and the inspection committee had to be very diplomatic in discouraging ponies which did not conform to the breed standard while not putting the breeders off the whole idea of registering ponies at all. Early judges often held differing opinions on what constituted a pony of correct Fell type, and this was clearly illustrated at the local Fell stallion show held at Middleton in Teesdale on 15 April 1920. The judges were Mr Tom Bainbridge from Brough and Mr R. B. Charlton from Hexham. They could not agree about which pony should win the class. Mr Bainbridge went for Sporting Times, a skewbald pony, while Mr Charlton favoured Hilton Fashion, a grey, as he contended that a piebald or skewbald could not be of pure Fell pony blood. At length, a third man was brought into the ring to adjudicate between the two ponies. The referee judge had been drinking in the local pub and was very much the worse for drink, but he staggered into the ring, swaying visibly. Without even looking at the ponies he pointed with his stick and in a loud drunken voice shouted 'Gee it to Baldie!' and that was that. Fortunately, drunken judges were as rare as coloured stallions winning and, gradually, the true Fell colours of black, brown, bay and grey were generally accepted. White markings of any kind did not debar a pony from being registered, but excessive white markings were discouraged as they suggested cross breeding somewhere in the pony's ancestry. Despite an inevitable small percentage of anomalies, the average height for the Fell pony remained consistent at 13.2 hh.

The National Pony Society's system of having an inspection committee in the north proved to have many failings, and the pony breeders themselves recognised the need for stricter enforcement of the registration rules if the true purebred Fell pony was to be fostered and encouraged. In 1912, a different committee was set up by a group of breeders in the north to be responsible for the welfare and registration of Fell ponies. The new northern committee, which in time would become the Fell Pony Society, was quite separate from the National Pony Society although the latter would continue to maintain the registration records for the breed as part of its stud book, a service it was to provide for the Fell Pony Society up until 1980. The fifth Earl of Lonsdale sat as president of the new committee with Mr F. W. Garnett of Windermere as secretary. The other members included representatives from Hesket New Market, Keswick, Shap, Appleby, Brough, Kirkby Stephen, Middleton and Sedbergh Agricultural Societies as well as two representatives from the National Pony Society. Mr Ed. de Vere Irving, a member of the Shap Agricultural Society, was elected chairman, with Mr R. W. Gibson of Orton vice chairman.

Under the direction of the secretary, Mr Garnett, who had been working towards the formation of a society for the breed since 1903, a scheme for the 'encouragement of Fell pony breeding' was formulated and approved by the Board of Agriculture which gave £150 for the committee to distribute as stallion premiums. After careful consideration, it was decided to award six premiums of £20 each to the stallion owners, plus half a crown for each foal born to his stallion. The owner was not to charge more than ten shillings stud fee plus half a crown for the groom, and stallions had to serve no more than fifty mares. The districts in which the premium stallions were to stand at stud were selected as being Hesket New Market, Keswick, Shap, Appleby, Kirkby Stephen and Middleton, and the premiums were to be awarded at the stallion shows held each spring in the respective areas. The local agricultural societies were allowed to nominate the judges who were then approved by the Fell Pony Committee. At both Hesket New Market and Appleby stallion shows, only one pony was exhibited, while at Kirkby Stephen there were only two entries, and the other shows only attracted four stallions each. Reviewing the success of the scheme at the end of the year, the secretary wrote: 'The number of mares served in some of the districts is disappointing, and is attributable to more than one cause. First the lack of advertising the rounds and fees of the premium stallions, second the late start made by some – caused by delay in registration and non-receipt of the service books.' Nevertheless, it was an encouraging start overall, with the number of mares served in each district ranging from twenty-three in the Hesket New Market area to the maximum of fifty in the Appleby area. Foaling returns were required by the secretary

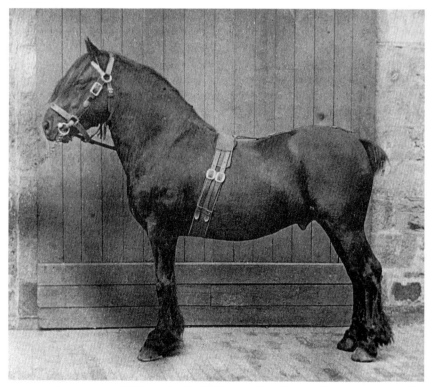

Mountain Ranger, foaled 1906, bred by Mr J. W. Dent of Middleton in Teesdale, and owned by Mr J. A. Bussey of Barnard Castle. Awarded the Board of Agriculture premium for Middleton in Teesdale in 1912.

who kept meticulous records of the colours of mares and foals, the numbers of breeding mares and stallions in the various areas, and other information which indicated trends within the breed. Writing in 1912 he observed: 'It is extremely desirable in a foundation breed, such as Fell ponies, to maintain as many mares of a black or brown colour as possible, both from a practical as well as from a Mendelian point of view.' As regards the breed population at that time he added:

> The number of Fell pony stallions in the district covered by the work of the committee as far as I know is thirty, and assuming that each of these served 36 mares each, the number of breeding mares in the district would be 1080. I have made this calculation to find out as nearly as possible the requirements of the district. It must be noted that these figures are probably underestimated, and that the district covered by the committee does not cover the entire Fell pony country.

A great many of the hill farms in the Lake District had grazing rights for both sheep and ponies on the open fell land, the number of animals which could be grazed being dictated by the size of the farm and its acreage of enclosed land. Traditionally, Fell ponies had been kept on this open high ground since time immemorial and they lived and bred in small family groups with the minimum of contact with man. Once a year the farmers helped each other to collect the ponies up and drive them down into the narrow walled lanes called 'outgans' which lead from the open fell to the fields or farms lower down. The word 'outgan' comes from the Norse term *at ganga* meaning 'to go', and is still much used in the north. Here the ponies were sorted out and the 'stags' or unbroken three year olds penned ready for sale while the rest were returned to the fells for another year. Soon after, the stags were driven in one loose-headed herd to one of the north country horse fairs like Brough Hill or Appleby, where each man claimed his ponies and penned them separately ready for inspection by potential customers.

Branding ponies for identification purposes was not common practice, although ear-marking by cutting slits or nicks in one ear was quite usual. Even so, disputes over ownership arose occasionally so each district elected an honorary umpire whose job it was to make a ruling decision regarding ownership in such cases. In order to do so, the umpire needed to know the ponies in the particular area he was responsible for. Some of the umpires, like Tommy Wharton of Tebay, who was responsible for Langdale and Wild Boar fells, were very knowledgeable men who made very few mistakes in identifying the young ponies.

For many years horse fairs like Brough Hill were literally a clearing house for the breed, as well as important social gatherings attracting farmers, horse dealers, gypsies, showmen, travelling people, fortune tellers, pick-pockets and petty thieves. For days prior to the fair, all the roads leading to Brough would be seething with gypsy caravans, brightly painted flat carts, herds of loose ponies grazing the roadsides as they came, and riders. Broad grass road verges were used as overnight camping sites by the travelling people who tethered their ponies in lines along the roads, and the local tradesmen, especially blacksmiths, enjoyed the extra business the fair brought. The fair was actually held in the centre of Brough originally, but recently the congestion and potential danger to spectators caused the police to move it out of the town centre to where there was more room. The ponies were penned or tied up along the roadside, and all transactions were privately conducted as there was no organised auction as in most sales. Prospective purchasers would ask to see the pony move and the vendor would 'flash' the animal by running it out in hand up and down the main street. Spectators who did not get out of the way quickly were in danger of being trodden as several ponies were trotted out at once, and accidents were quite common. Even today, the old-fashioned tradition of 'flashing' ponies to show their action can still be seen at Appleby Horse Fair. Most of the stags were bought by dealers who took them home, broke them in to drive and occasionally to ride, and sold them on to the big colliery companies or tradesmen seeking a good delivery pony.

Even before the First World War, the secretary of the Fell Pony Committee commented that the breeding of ponies on the fell in a semi-wild state was becoming a thing of the past. The system was no good for farmers who used their ponies regularly around the farm but who might expect their mares to breed a foal every year in addition. It was these small breeders who were the first to benefit from the Committee's stallion premium scheme, which was based on the old tradition of travelling stallions, a system dating back several centuries.

The idea of travelling stallions was born out of necessity. In rural areas like the Lake District farmers with just one or two mares were posed with a problem when it came to getting their mares covered each spring. With no motorised horse transport, the farmer would have to lead, ride or drive the mare wherever the stallion stood and, as many of the farms were in isolated or inaccessible areas, this could mean a long journey and a day or more wasted at a busy time of the farming year. If the mare had a foal at foot a journey of more than a few miles was out of the question. It is also unlikely that the stallion owner would want a lot of visiting mares on his limited acreage because of the damage they would do to the ground, especially in wet weather. Consequently, stallion owners 'travelled' their ponies. Setting off on the second Monday in May, the stallion's owner or groom would lead the pony on a planned route around the local region, stopping at those farms where the stallion's services were required. As well as paying a stud fee, the mare's owner was expected to provide lodging overnight for the stallion man plus a field or stable for the pony if his farm was the last one visited that day. The next day the stallion would be taken on to the next farm, sometimes calling at two farms in the day, and the route would be repeated each week until the end of the season, which was traditionally August Bank Holiday Monday. After the season, the stallion might have been used for general work around the farm or turned out on the open fell to winter.

In order for a stallion to be awarded a premium, it had to receive a veterinary certificate of soundness. Highland Fashion's certificate for 1913, when he travelled as a premium stallion, read:

> This is to certify that the Fell pony stallion named Highland Fashion, the property of Messrs. J. and R. Bellas of Moor Farm, Keswick, has after veterinary examination been accepted by the Board of Agriculture and Fisheries as sound and suitable for breeding purposes and has been placed on their register of stallions for the registration year ending 31st October 1913. Its identification marks are: Black with small white star. Signed and sealed this 7th day of January 1913.
>
> F. W. Garnett, M.R.C.V.S., Windermere, and A. W. Anstruther, Assistant Secretary.

Hereditary unsoundness was, and still is, unknown in the Fell pony. Many of the stallions used for travelling started their annual tour in soft and unfit condition but the endless miles of steady walking soon hardened them up and guaranteed that they were in peak physical condition by the end of the season. A fit stallion usually maintained a high fertility rate and this was important, as frequent return visits to a mare who kept returning to season were not always feasible. The stamina and constitution of the stallion was also put to the test by the weekly distances walked, often on rough tracks or across open moorland, and in all weathers. A stallion in good condition and well turned out was also its own advertisement, and some stallions became great favourites with the local people as they travelled in the district. Above all, the system was self-regulating as good stallions which got well were in demand while poorer quality ponies were not.

A typical route was that travelled by the stallion, Lingcropper Again, at the turn of the century:

MONDAY Winton, Brough, Stainmore, Warcop, Musgrave, to Mr Harrison's at Blandsworth for the night.
TUESDAY Soulby, Little Asby, Newbiggin, to Mr Bradbury's at Ravenstonedale for the night.
WEDNESDAY Fell End, Cautley, Sedbergh, to Mr Aitrigg's at Garsdale for the night.
THURSDAY Mallerstang, Nateby, Kirkby Stephen, then back to Mr Harrison's at Blandsworth where he remained until the following Monday.

Weekly itineraries like the one above were only guidelines and would be altered to suit individual mare owners. Lingcropper Again's stud card read: 'The route will be arranged to suit parties requiring Lingcropper Again's services.'

Many of the men who travelled the stallions were characters in their own right. They had to endure the indifferent hospitality they received at some of their overnight stops. At some the food was dreadful, at others they had to sleep in the same bed as the farmer and his family, or even bed down in the stable with the pony. One famous stallion traveller of years ago was said to have been more productive in the district he travelled than the stallion!

Small printed stud cards giving details of the stallion were handed out along the route. These gave details of the stallion's breeding, age, stud fee and weekly route plus any relevant additional information regarding show wins, trotting speeds, or notable progeny. The stud card for Heltondale Victor recorded his virtues in verse:

Here comes Heltondale Victor,
We know him by his walk,
This is the horse that goes so well,
And makes the people talk.
Look at his head, his neck, his eyes,
Mark well his shape and size,
Superior action he displays,
Amazing strength likewise.

Any complaints about a premium stallion or his handler or the route they travelled had to be addressed to the committee representative for that area or to the secretary of the Fell Pony Committee.

One of the first Fell stallions to be travelled on a regular planned route was a pony called King of the Country, who was bought by Mr Winder of Caldbeck in 1876 and travelled in the northern part of Cumberland by his owner. Although a few stallions were ridden or driven, Mr Winder having one called Royal Star which was driven in a sulky, most were led and the stallion men and their charges were a common sight in rural areas every spring as they walked on their rounds. In order not to hinder progress, the very minimum of belongings was carried by the stallion man, often only a rolled up raincoat fastened to the pony's surcingle and a few personal necessities stuffed into the pockets.

The system of travelling stallions began to decline as the demand for ponies started to fade in the years following the First World War, and the availability of motorised horse transport only furthered the gradual demise of the travelling men as they were known. A few die-hards hung on to the old ways, and the last Fell stallion to be travelled was a black pony called Master John who, with his owner Joseph Baxter of Threlkeld, trod the roads around Keswick in 1948.

In his report to the Fell Pony Committee in 1914 the secretary, Frank Garnett, wrote:

> The attention of breeders of Fell ponies is directed to the breeding of the premium and many of the other Fell pony stallions in the district. Of the five premium stallions all without exception are descended on their sire's or their dam's side from Blooming Heather and the time is fast approaching when the question of introducing fresh blood must be faced. It must be borne in mind that the Highland pony, i.e. the original Galloway, and our own, now called the Fell pony, are of one and the same foundation breed, and the interchange of stallions between the two districts in which they are bred has been continued since time out of mind. In seeking new blood again, the selection of the very best and purest blacks or browns of these ponies would seem to be indicated.

Despite his suggestion, no appreciable amount of alien blood was introduced with the intention of improving the Fell pony. However, the use of Fell blood to produce new breeds or types or to improve existing stock was widespread. Hunters, polo ponies, chargers, artillery pack animals and tradesmen's driving cobs had all at some time or other benefited from the introduction of a little Fell pony blood.

Two quite distinct breeds of pony were direct off-shoots from the Fell, the Dales and the Hackney pony. The former was produced to meet the demand for a stronger,

Mr Joe Baxter of Threlkeld with the stallion Master John, the last Fell stallion to be 'travelled' in Cumbria.

heavier type of pony better suited to working in the valleys or 'dales', while the lighter Fell continued to be used for shepherding and light farm work on the hills or 'fells'. Clydesdale blood was introduced to Fell pony stock and the resulting progeny, the fore-runners of the Dales breed, attained the size and strength required by the farmers who predominated in the dales to the east of the Pennine range and who favoured the larger type of pony. Although Dales ponies to this day conform to the accepted Fell colours of black, brown, bay and grey, white markings are far more common than in the Fell and can be attributed to the Clydesdale influence. Pony character and quality were also sacrificed for size and strength and, although the

69

Dales earned great popularity for itself in the northeastern counties where it is still bred, the true Fell pony breeding stock continued in its pure form on the moors and hill farms of the Lake District. For many years ponies out of Dales mares and by Fell stallions were acceptable for the Dales pony register, although Dales blood in Fells was frowned upon by the purists of the Fell breed.

The Hackney pony was developed first as a type and then by careful selection and a shrewd breeding policy as a breed in the 1870s. It owed its origins to one man, Christopher W. Wilson of Rigmaden Park, near Kirkby Lonsdale in Westmorland, who was a brilliant, innovative but enigmatic man. Those who could remember him described him as quick tempered, passionately dedicated to whatever interested him at the time, but equally liable suddenly to lose interest and turn his attention to something completely different. Rigmaden was one of the first country houses in England to have electric light, Wilson was one of the first people to farm trout commercially, he invented the Wilson snaffle driving bit, and he was famous for his unusual pets which included a badger, an otter and a monkey. It was said that he once bought an elephant but his wife would not allow him to bring it home. He experimented with the use of silos for the storage of winter fodder, and was one of the first Englishmen involved in agriculture to recognise the values of Friesian cattle which he subsequently imported from Holland. There was also a deer park at Rigmaden where various species of deer were kept including red, roe, fallow, wapiti from North America and Sika deer from Asia, and he kept a flock of Suffolk sheep which, at that time, were a little-known breed in the north of England.

Christopher Wilson began breeding ponies with the aim of producing a harness pony with quality, substance, and stamina, extravagant action and great presence and, most importantly, plenty of pony character. He specifically did not want to produce a horse breed. He began by selecting a small number of purebred Fell pony mares, and he travelled extensively all over Cumberland and Westmorland to find exactly what he wanted. The stallion he used on these mares, Sir George, came from Yorkshire and was directly descended from the old Norfolk Roadster. Standing barely fourteen hands, his illustrious pedigree included such names as Sportsman, his sire; Phenomenon, the amazing trotting mare; and Flying Childers. Foaled in 1866, Sir George's impressive looks and tremendous action had earned him great success in the showring, and he had won first prize at eight consecutive shows of the Royal Agricultural Society. The progeny of Sir George and the Fell mares inherited their sire's excellent stamp of conformation and extravagant action, and the substance and congenital stamina of their dams. Most of them were bay. In order to keep the size down, Wilson turned the first cross and subsequent generations of youngstock out onto the Rigmaden moors to live as their Fell ancestors had done, and none of the ponies he bred ever exceeded fourteen hands. By careful line breeding back to Sir George, the 'Wilson pony', as it was originally known, was established and sufficiently well-known by 1905 that one of the magazines of the time, *The Horse*, published an article on it. It was described as existing in small numbers and having been founded on a long sustained cross between the Hackney and the Fell pony. Such famous ponies as Little Wonder and Sir Horace, who was virtually unbeaten in the showring, were bred at Rigmaden.

In a very short time, Wilson had laid the foundations for what would become known as the Hackney pony. Then, at the height of his glory, Wilson went down to his stables one morning and told his stud groom, Bob Moffat, that he was selling all his ponies. Being a progressive and forward-thinking man, it is possible that he foresaw the end of horsepower as a means of transport and felt there was no future for his new breed of harness pony. This would seem to be supported by the fact that Christopher Wilson owned the first car in Westmorland, registered EC 1, and he obviously recognised the impact that motor cars were to have on the horse world in the coming years. A dispersal sale was held a short time later and all his stock was sold at prices which were quite astronomical in those days. The best of the ponies were sold to the Marquis of Londonderry, Lord Daresbury and Sir Humphrey de Trafford, the latter also employing the services of Bob Moffat. When Sir Humphrey sold out by public auction in September 1895, six of his ponies bred by Christopher Wilson averaged £720 each, and a yearling filly made 900 guineas. Some of the ponies went to William Hollins of Mansfield who, in turn, also employed Moffat. Wilson never took an interest in ponies again.

The potential of the Fell pony as foundation stock for creating other breeds or types had been recognised by Christopher Wilson's grandfather, also of the same name, who was a partner in a bank in Kendal and who bought Rigmaden in 1823. He used Fell mares to produce a type of animal known as the turf pony. Before grandstands became a standard provision at race courses, turf ponies were to be seen at most race meetings. Rather than watch the race from the rails or from the top of a coach or char-a-banc which was the usual practice, owners, spectators and even representatives from the press mounted on turf ponies would take up a position on the rails and gallop alongside the runners for as long as possible. This necessitated a pony that had tremendous stamina coupled with weight-carrying ability, as many of the riders were portly gentlemen. For the same reason, a pony that was not too big facilitated mounting and dismounting, and an animal that was a comfortable ride was an added bonus. A large number of turf ponies were bred in the north from Fell stock and then sold out of the region. Although the sporting artists of the day painted innumerable racing scenes or individual portraits of famous or favourite racehorses, the turf pony was very rarely recorded on canvas. An exception is the painting of an unnamed turf pony bred by Christopher Wilson and showing a weight-carrying stamp of docked gelding very obviously bred from Fell pony stock. Painted by S. Marshall and engraved in 1828, the painting is significant as it verifies the use of Fell blood in the production of this now virtually forgotten type of riding pony. Although the Fell is not noted for its galloping speed, one exceptional pony, Perfect Model, won a one mile flat race open to ponies under fourteen hands at Emly near Wakefield!

Although Dales pony breeders regularly used Fells to improve their stock by re-establishing the pony quality lost through crossing with the Clydesdale, Fells were also successfully used to improve other British native breeds. There is evidence to suggest that both the Highland and New Forest pony breeds benefited at one time from a small infusion of Fell blood, while many top class Welsh ponies at the turn of the century were sired by a black Fell stallion standing little more than thirteen hands called Linnel Don. This remarkable pony was a big winner in harness classes and was described by the famous pony breeder, William Foster of the Mel Valley stud, as 'the best harness pony living at his height'. His innumerable wins included the Welsh National, the Royal Show in 1906, and second prize in the class for ponies in harness, not exceeding fourteen hands, at the first International Horse Show at Olympia in 1907. He was owned by the Duchess of Newcastle and his most notable progeny included his daughter, Clumber Blacky, and his granddaughter, Clumber Starlight. Commenting on the use of one native breed to improve another, Linnel Don's breeder, Roy B. Charlton, said:

An infusion of real pony blood from one pure mountain breed to another mountain pony breed can produce real ponies. Go far enough back in the history of Britain's native ponies, and it will be found that they were all one stock. Environment, purposes for which they have been required, and local fashion, over a very long time has divided the ponies into different types, but provided you select from the purest of the different breeds, you will find that such good samples of each breed are very similar when seen together.

In an attempt to improve the draught and pack animals of the country, a number of

Fell stallions were shipped to Pakistan in the 1940s, including a three-year-old black colt, Dalemain Knight of the Thistle, bred by Mrs B. K. McCosh of Penrith. The colt's half sister, being out of the same mare, was Windsor Gipsy, the mare owned and driven by HRH Princess Elizabeth. The Fell ponies were crossed on to local Pakistani mares to produce animals with more substance and strength without increasing the height or losing the inherent hardiness and quiet disposition. In the late 1940s, a consignment of Fell stallions was also sent to North Africa, again for the purpose of improving the local stock, and in 1951 the secretary of the Fell Pony Society received an enquiry about the possibility of taking Fell ponies to Basutoland in South Africa.

The Spanish Royal Commission, which was not dissimilar to the Ministry of Agriculture in this country, also took a keen interest in Fell ponies, having seen examples of the breed exhibited at the London pony shows in the 1920s. They subsequently bought a young Linnels bred stallion for the sum of £200, a good price in those days, and were sufficiently impressed with the animal to return and purchase another twenty-eight more Fell stallions from the same stud over a period of time. Some years after the first Fells were bought by the Spanish government, Roy Charlton, who had bred and sold the ponies, was at San Sebastian in northern Spain. He asked a local horseman if he knew the whereabouts of any of the young ponies bred from the pony mares of the region and by British pony stallions. The man told him where he could find them in large numbers and Mr Charlton travelled up into the mountain country to the south of San Sebastian to see them. He remembered:

> There they were, lots of them, all either black or dark brown in colour, and so unlike their dams that there wasn't the slightest doubt in the minds of my wife, my son and myself, who saw them, about these young ponies being the progeny of the Fell sires I had sold to the Spanish Government. The pony mares were all of one type, they all showed definite Barb features, and were chesnut or grey or light bay in colour, yet their off-spring were black or dark brown in colour. These youngsters had plenty of bone and substance and showed a lot of Fell pony type.

The success of the exported Fell pony stallions encouraged private buyers in Spain as well as Spaniards in Argentina to buy Fells, although these were not necessarily used to improve existing stock in those countries. Similarly, Fells were exported to a number of other countries in Europe and further afield, and in 1950 a stallion was lent to a stud in Germany for the season as part of an experimental breeding programme with the ultimate aim of upgrading the quality and performance of the local stock.

6 The foundation of the Fell Pony Society

In the spring of 1916, the 'Fell Pony Committee for Cumberland, Westmorland and North Yorkshire' met at the Crown Hotel in Penrith for their annual meeting. It was proposed by Mr R. B. Charlton that a society be formed to 'promote the breeding of high class riding and driving ponies', a suggestion that got the approval of the other members present, who included in their number Messrs Garnett, Henry Holme from Thrimby who was a descendant of the ancient kings of Mardale, R. Dent, and E. de Vere Irving. They saw the need to continue encouraging the improvement and registration of ponies to maintain the purity of the breed, and they felt this would be best achieved by forming a society and inviting those persons interested in the Fell pony to join.

The problems encountered as a result of the war postponed the formation of the Society until 1918, but did not prevent the committee continuing to submit a stallion scheme to the Board of Agriculture each year for approval. In 1916, the number of premiums offered to travelling Fell stallions was reduced to five, although the value of each premium had increased to £40 with approximately £4 added on at a rate of half a crown for each foal born, the average being thirty-two to each stallion. The first £15 of the premium was paid at the time of the award, the balance being paid at the close of the service season. A total of twenty-three stallions contested the premiums at the district stallion shows at Appleby, Kirkby Stephen, Middleton in Teesdale, Keswick and Shap. Two years earlier, the number of exhibits at the shows had been thirty-eight and, in reviewing the 1916 season, the secretary commented that 'the season had been a most difficult one to work, both for the committee and the stallion owners through curtailed railway service and shortage of labour. In one instance, the owner of a premium stallion had to travel the horse himself, in a district far removed from his home, leaving his wife, single handed, on his 100 acre farm – his only son being taken for the war.'

A casualty of the war was the brood mare premium scheme originally submitted to the Board of Agriculture in 1914. The Board had agreed to offer small premiums for registered Fell mares at each of six affiliated Agricultural Society shows. No mare could get more than one premium and to be eligible she had to be registered herself and in foal to a registered stallion. Unfortunately, the brood mare premiums were short-lived as, owing to the war, no agricultural shows were held where the premiums could be offered. Concluding his annual report for 1918, the secretary, Mr Garnett, wrote: 'The season has been the most difficult one to work which the Society has experienced, and I trust before another one comes around the war will have been brought to a victorious conclusion.' His optimism proved correct and the following year the mare premiums were reinstated. The stallion premium scheme was re-organised and updated with an increase in the number of regions to be travelled by stallions, backed up by a more effective administrative system. To be eligible for the balance of the premium paid at the end of the season, the stallion owner had to keep a record book supplied for the purpose in which he had to enter the names of all the mares covered by his entire. The book then had to be returned to the Board at the end of August.

The importance of publicising the breed, especially outside the Fell pony's indigenous home area, was also recognised by the newly formed Fell Pony Society. In 1916, they had been invited by the National Pony Society to send a group of Fells down to their show in London where they were offering prizes for the best group of not less than three ponies from any of the native breeds. Although the advertising value of exhibiting a group of Fells at this most prestigious show was not in doubt, the secretary, Mr Garnett, was compelled to concede that 'The expense of sending such a group up to London was far beyond the resources of this committee.' However, he was surprised and delighted to receive a letter from Mr G. Norris Midwood, one of the National Pony Society's representatives to the Fell Pony Society, reading:

Dear Garnett,
     Read the enclosed – I think the Fells should be represented and offer to pay expenses of one or two groups if you can arrange it.
                         Yours, G. Norris Midwood

A special meeting was called at which it was decided to accept the generous offer of sponsorship. It was also resolved that the group should consist of one stallion and two mares, the selection of which was to be left to the chairman and secretary. Unfortunately, when the selection day came around, Mr E. de Vere Irving, the chairman, was ill in bed and his place was taken by Mr Holme, a well-known breeder. He and the secretary travelled over 100 miles in appalling weather conditions, including snow a foot deep on Shap fell, to select the ponies. In the end they chose Mr J. Relph's Glengarry, a black grandson of Blooming Heather, Mr Mallinson's Bella II, and the Earl of Lonsdale's Hoo-Poe. Reviewing the success of the venture after the show, Mr Garnett wrote:

Glengarry, foaled 1911. Owned by Mr J. Relph, Shap. Awarded the Board of Agriculture premium for the Appleby district in 1914.

There were thirteen groups shown in this class in March and representing Dartmoor, Exmoor, Fell, Highland, New Forest and Welsh ponies, and the judges awarded the champion prize to group four 'Fell', and also awarded the £50 special challenge trophy, offered by the proprietors of Country Life, a solid silver replica of a James I Salt, for the best pony in the above class to Mr J. Relph's Fell pony stallion, Glengarry. It is worthy of note that he received the trophy from the hands of Queen Alexandra, and he also received the silver medal from the Society. Lord Lonsdale was good enough to leave his share of the prize money, £4, in my hands for the benefit of the committee.

On 10 October 1922, the committee of the Fell Pony Society met at the Crown Hotel in Penrith for their annual meeting and decided to 'reform itself on a more liberal constitution'. Up until then, the committee had consisted of representatives from each district travelled by a premium stallion plus a handful of co-opted members, and two representatives from the National Pony Society who were responsible for liaison between the two societies. At this meeting the whole committee resigned and a new committee was elected. The reformation of the Society was instigated by a number of events, foremost of which was the grievous loss of the honorary secretary and treasurer, Frank Garnett, who died unexpectedly earlier in the year. His contribution to the breed by playing a key role in the formation of a society for the Fell pony was tremendous, as it is questionable whether or not the breed would have survived the years between the wars without the backing of a patron society. Another major change was that the distribution of government grants for the assistance of horse breeding was transferred from the Ministry of Agriculture to the War Office. At that time, the continued use of cavalry in military operations was not in doubt and, in taking administrative responsibility for the premiums, the War Office was acknowledging the role of the larger native breeds including the Fell in the breeding of troop horses. Lastly, the Society discussed for the first time the possibility of amalgamating the regional stallion shows to produce a better show of ponies and attract more publicity for the breed. Although the suggestion was well received, it was not until two years later that the new secretary, Mr A. W. Wingate, announced that there would be one central show held at Penrith in conjunction with the Penrith Agricultural Society's Colt and Stallion Show in 1924, to which all stallions wishing to compete would be sent and a premium awarded for each district.

One of the primary aims of the Society was still to achieve consistency of type throughout the breed and, at this time, a resolution was passed which stipulated that in future the height for mares in the stud book would be reduced from 14.0 hh to 13.2 hh. Of the ponies registered in 1922, forty-five were brown, forty were black, and nine were bay. There were five greys, one piebald, and one described as 'black-dun'.

White markings were also considerably fewer than they had been in earlier years, so evidently the efforts of the committee were working to encourage the true Fell type and to discourage those animals not conforming to the breed standard.

The war years had taken their toll, however, for, although Fell ponies were officially too small to be commandeered by the War Office, a large number had been sold for meat, much of it for human consumption. As the country readjusted after several years at war, the prices for Fell ponies took a serious, if temporary, slump. Before the war, a broken pony could be bought for £20–30; a typical mare and foal making 35 guineas for the pair in 1905. Some years later, a consignment of ponies was sold off the hill at Brampton and their prices reflected the fact that they would be unhandled and probably wild. In-foal mares of between four and eight years made up to 16 guineas, foals up to 6 guineas, yearlings and two year olds up to 8 guineas, and unbroken three year olds or 'stags' up to 11½ guineas. Immediately after the war when prices fell dramatically, a good broken mare could be bought for a few pounds quite easily. By 21 October 1922, when Mr H. Watson of Uldale sold his entire stud of forty-six ponies by public auction, trade had recovered sufficiently well for the sale to attract a large number of buyers. As a report of the time confirmed, 'the spirited bidding testified to the popularity of the breed. The ponies were brought direct from the fell into the sale ring, and the following prices were obtained: Foals, up to 19 guineas; two year olds, up to 32 guineas; brood mares up to 50 guineas.'

Membership of the Society was increasing very slowly, although in 1923 twenty-nine new members joined the Society. Despite this, the breeding stock of the Fell pony still remained almost exclusively in the hands of hill farmers situated in and around the Lake District. The Society was still campaigning to persuade breeders to register their stock, and the stipulation that only registered ponies were eligible for the premiums offered at many of the local shows was an encouragement. As Mr Wingate commented, 'the classes for Fell ponies at the local shows are becoming increasingly popular, and are now the leading feature in the horse section'. At Penrith show in 1923, fifty-three Fell ponies were exhibited. Four years later, there were seventy-five Fells shown in their respective classes at the same show. A commentator wrote: 'the premiums given at our local shows by the National Pony Society for the best Fell pony brood mares registered or eligible for registration are very much appreciated. These premiums bring out new ponies, and very frequently owners who are also new to the Fell Pony Society.'

When Mr R. B. Charlton took over the secretaryship of the Society in 1927, he was aware of the importance of marketing the breed both locally by encouraging the

agricultural shows to include Fell pony classes in their schedules, and nationally by ensuring that Fells were exhibited at the prestigious London shows. Compared to other native breeds like the Welsh and Dartmoor, the Fell was still relatively unknown outside its traditional breeding ground and, despite the expense and trouble of transporting ponies to the capital, the rewards in terms of the extensive publicity and interest shown in the ponies were well justified. Mr Charlton had shown ponies at the National Pony Society show at Islington each March for many years with considerable success. He had set a precedent by showing his Fells neither clipped nor trimmed, although it was not until some time later that the National Pony Society had ruled that mountain and moorland ponies were to be shown in their natural state. One of Mr Charlton's most successful ponies was Linnel Lingcropper, a black pony whose pedigree could be traced back to Old Lingcropper and the famous Blooming Heather. Linnel Lingcropper won extensively in the showring, including first prize at the Royal Show, the championship cup at Islington, the King George V special, and several War Office premiums.

Moor Lad, foaled in 1923, owned by Mr J. Bellas of Keswick. First and reserve champion at the National Pony Society show, London, 1927.

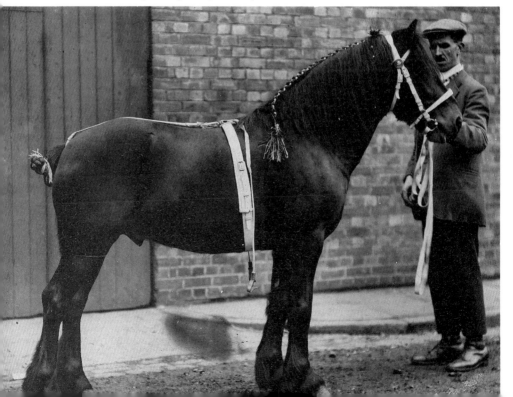

Instigated by Mr Charlton, the Society agreed that it would be advantageous to the breed if more Fells were shown at the NPS London Show and, in 1929, the following advertisement appeared in the *Penrith and Cumberland Herald:* 'Will persons who wish to send ponies to the London Show in March please communicate with the honorary secretary, Mr R. B. Charlton, The Linnels, Hexham.'

The Society decided not only to arrange the rail transport to London for suitable ponies but planned to offer travel grants in addition as a further encouragement. The Society was also instrumental in persuading the Royal Show, held at Harrogate in 1929, to include a class for the best Fell brood mare with foal at foot in its schedule. The generous prize money, £15 first, £10 second, and £5 third, was an encouragement to breeders to exhibit their stock and the class was well patronised.

Evaluating the success of the society in achieving its aims, the secretary wrote:

Fell breeders have certainly enjoyed an extremely interesting and busy time; and our ponies have probably reached a higher standard of perfection than has been known since the formation of the Society, and in this they remain absolutely pure Fell pony. There have been no introductions of foreign blood; no attempts to produce something just a little bigger, or a little less, by an outcross to some other breed.

Our stallion parade, which is held at Penrith in April of each year, is becoming better and better, and this year it was quite wonderful to see the older pony stallions having to stand to one side to make room for the young strangers that were there to take the premiums. These beautiful young ponies are bound to further improve our Fell pony stock.

With the object of encouraging our owners to keep their well-bred and good looking entire colts we now have classes at the Penrith Spring show for yearling and two year old entire colts. This year these two classes brought forward 20 high class colts. Competition was very keen and the general tone was in the right direction.

Sales of Fell ponies have been better than usual. We know that nothing stimulates production more than good sales. Linnel Heather, Linnel Glen, Wait and See, Blencathra, Jack's Delight, Good Hope, Linnel Moor Boy, Linnel Snip, Wallthwaite Ranger, John Bradley, Bousfield John Bull, Linnel Boy, Minstrel Boy, Mosstrooper II, and other famous Fell pony stallions have been sold to go abroad. The trade for weight carrying ponies has never been so good.

Fell ponies of about 13.2 hh and up to weight over rough ground are going into the Scotch deer forests and elsewhere in numbers.

All this is very encouraging to the breeder, and the result is that the best colts are being kept entire, and the other ponies that are not wanted for stud are being taught to ride at home, instead of being driven to Brough Hill Fair in herds at 2½ years of age, and given away as they used to be for other people to make into profit.

Despite Roy Charlton's encouraging words, within a few years the depression of the 1930s coupled with the increased use of motorised power on the land would threaten the breed again by drastically reducing the market for these ponies. The days of great shooting parties on Scottish estates were fast diminishing along with the need for large numbers of shooting ponies, and tractors were becoming more common, even on hill farms, than the all-round farm pony – a role the Fell had filled for many generations. The Society chairman, Mr T. Holme, was still optimistic when he said: 'It is the duty of the Fell Pony Society to do its very best to maintain the improved standard of the Fell pony. We have a breed of pony second to none and with the continuing help of the Light Horse Breeding Department of the War Office we should continue to improve the native pony of Westmorland and Cumberland.' Unbeknown to him as he spoke, the War Office had already decided and were shortly to announce that, with the diminishing value of cavalry in favour of motorised army transportation, it would be unable to offer grants for stallion premiums any longer. The announcement came as a very severe blow to the Society, although the secretary expressed his hope that stallion owners would still be willing to travel their stallions the following season, 1932, even though no cash premiums could be offered. The lack of a financial incentive plus the substantially decreased demand for the services of a stallion did not justify the time and effort spent by the handlers travelling an entire, and interest waned dramatically. At the 1932 stallion show, only three stallions paraded, a sharp contrast to the well-filled classes of previous years.

Fearing for the future of the breed, Roy Charlton suggested to the National Trust that, as the Fell pony was part of our national heritage, they should start a small select stud of quality ponies to ensure that a purebred nucleus of ponies would survive whatever happened elsewhere. Although it was not National Trust policy to keep livestock, they were evidently sufficiently concerned about the possible disappearance of the breed altogether to be persuaded. Under the auspices of the Society, a number of ponies of correct type with good bloodlines were selected. They were kept

on National Trust ground at Gowbarrow Hall, near Ullswater, and the stud prefix of 'Gowbarrow' was adopted for all Fell ponies bred by the Trust.

Although financial restrictions made it difficult, the Society endeavoured to continue sending ponies down to the National Pony Society show in London each March as they felt that publicity for the breed was essential if it was to survive the lean years it was experiencing. A Society sub-committee, known as the London Show Committee, selected the ponies to go to Islington, and the cost of sending one pony to London was estimated to be £21 6s 3d.

Occasional anomalies still turned up among the registrations and at the Fell Pony Society spring meeting in March 1931 the secretary sought the advice of the council on whether or not he should have registered a chestnut foal whose parents were both registered. The filly, which also had a white blaze, was registered as being out of a black mare by a brown stallion. Although the council were evidently suspect of the foal's breeding, they agreed that on this occasion they were obliged to approve the registration.

In 1934, Roy Charlton regretfully resigned as secretary due to business commitments, and his place was taken by Mr Joseph Relph from Threlkeld, near Keswick, who bred many good ponies at his Birkett Bank stud. Lack of finance continued to prevent the Society from doing as much as it would have liked, and Mr Relph used to say that it was the donations to the Society from King George V that saved the Fell pony during those bleak years. Another avid supporter of the breed whose contributions were much appreciated was Mrs Heelis, a local landowner and conservationist, better known as the children's authoress, Beatrix Potter.

The same year, and contrary to previous policies, the War Office was able to make a one-off payment to the Society of £130 to be used for breeding premiums. Made up to £150 with £10 from Society funds and £10 kindly donated by the National Pony Society, the Society was able to offer four premiums of £37 10s each to stallions, and this was much appreciated by the stalwart breeders. At the time there was no profit at all in breeding ponies and it was only interest in preserving the Fell that kept enthusiasts breeding ponies. The War Office continued to give small grants, year to year, up until 1939 when the Racecourse Betting Control Board stepped in with a grant of £300 for travelling Fell stallions. After careful consideration, the Society allocated this in five regional premiums of £60, and the areas chosen were Middleton in Teesdale, Kirkby Stephen, Shap, Keswick and Appleby. Although the Betting Control Board grant was given every year, the annual amount could not be guaranteed and was never consistent. In 1940, the grant was down to £75 and the five

83

premiums were only worth £15 each. In order to get maximum benefit from the premium money, the Society reviewed the premiums and districts each year, taking into account the number of registered mares covered in each district, the number of foals born, the colours of the foals and the number registered.

Among the notable ponies having influence on the breed during the 1930s, one of the best known was a 13.3 hh black stallion foaled in 1933 and called Storm Boy. He was owned and travelled by Mr Joe Baxter from Threlkeld, and he was by a pony called Bob Silvertail whose distinguishing feature was his grey tail, the rest of his body being black. Bob Silvertail was also notable for his unpredictable and vicious nature, most unusual in a Fell, and he was eventually sent to work in Kentmere Quarries where it was hoped that the hard repetitious work might quieten him down. Although he was difficult with everyone else, the quarry foreman's young daughter seemed to have an empathy with the stallion and she could do anything with him. Both Bob Silvertail and his more famous son, Storm Boy, produced many very good ponies, and some of today's top showring winners can trace their ancestry back to these ponies.

In 1936, the first Fell gelding was registered. In subsequent volumes of the stud book other geldings were registered, including a total of fourteen in Volume XXVI as the value of registering other than just breeding stock was recognised.

Fell pony gelding, Baldersdale Hero. In recent years the demand for broken Fell geldings has risen substantially.

Fell classes continued to be staged at local agricultural shows. Recalling the Lakeland shows of the 1930s in an article for the Fell Pony Society, Grace Teasdale, whose family bred the Longlands ponies, wrote:

During these years we showed ponies at five local shows: Ireby, Hesket New Market, Cockermouth, Haweswater and Keswick. The ponies were walked there and back – often starting before first light and coming back to the farm long after dark. I remember well the stalwarts of that generation: John Bellas, who showed his Moor Daisies with such flair and expertise; Jim Wilson, who brought a string of attractive ponies from Haltcliffe; Joseph Fawcett with Besses and Madges from Longlands; Willie Winder from Caldbeck and Fellside with his famous roans, and Dick Little from Guards, a breeder who knows a 'good un'. In 1928, Joseph Fawcett and Willie Winder made the journey to the London Pony Show with Longlands Bess and Mountain Jester. Above all we remember Joseph Baxter who for so long walked his stallions either over or around Skiddaw, stabled overnight with us at Longlands and walked over by Fellside, Faulds, Caldbeck and Haltcliffe to Threlkeld the next day. Through those lean hard years he never gave up and was unfailingly cheerful, patient and skilled in the work.

When the foals were weaned there was more walking. All the ponies were gathered in from the fell. The foals were kept in a large shed. The rest were taken (walked) to lower land at Wythmoor near Workington for the winter. They were brought back in early April in time to go to the fell to foal. The foals were fed twice a day and allowed on the fell for exercise and water every day but were housed at night.

Petrol rationing during the war years resulted in a temporary revival in the use of Fell ponies on the land and in harness, but the revival was short-lived and, with the coming of peace, motor vehicles again took precedence.

The difficulties of the war years had not prevented the Fell Pony Society from instigating and operating a new inspection scheme which was introduced with the aim of getting more ponies registered. The rules for registration of ponies were reviewed and amended in the 1940s, and a new rule brought in which stated that 'If only one parent is registered or if the pony's pedigree is unknown, the pony must be passed by an inspector appointed by the Fell Pony Society. Piebalds, skewbalds and chestnuts are debarred.' The scheme would prevent good animals of true Fell type which were not registered being lost to the Society, and its introduction was met with approval and enthusiasm by the breeders, many of whom were hill farmers who had bred ponies for years but never bothered with the paperwork necessary to register them.

An inspection committee consisting of Messrs Relph, Bellas and Charlton, junior, was elected by the Society at this time. Mrs Sylvia McCosh, who was helping Mr Relph with the secretarial work and who was later to be officially elected assistant secretary, undertook most of the clerical work connected with the scheme including accompanying the inspectors when they went out. She later wrote:

Our chief problem was covering great distances, with petrol rationing still operational, in order to inspect mares for registration. Joseph Relph and I planned some lengthy expeditions, and we hired Mr Aldersea's taxi from Blencowe, near Penrith. We drove across Shap fells, our first call being at Roundthwaite Bridge, near Tebay, where Tommy Thompson, always to be seen wearing leather leggings and a pork pie hat, met us with two lovely black mares, one being Sybil, the mother of Roundthwaite Lucky Jim. He and other breeders walked some distances to meet us at this particular point, all eager to have their ponies registered. I had previously written to all possible breeders to arrange these meetings and save petrol. We saw James Ewbank's ponies in Ravenstonedale, and on we travelled to see Norman Handley's ponies at Haygarth in the wild Sedbergh country – some of these had become very part-bred with the necessities of wartime.

Other expeditions followed. Roy Charlton and I toured the Grasmere and Rydal area. We went to Shap and to Orton and I was introduced to innumerable pony men of great knowledge. Dr Anthony Metcalfe-Gibson, who lived in a charming house in Orton, owned one of the most beautiful mares I have ever seen, dark brown and full of quality and substance. We sought out Willie Winder who we found ploughing on the high ground on Low Fellside. Climbing out of the Caldbeck Valley, we went on to Wigton to visit old Mr Bell at Bank House, and back to Guardhouse at Threlkeld where Joe Baxter was in fine form and about to start another season travelling his stallion, Storm Boy.

Before the end of the war, the breed standard was reappraised but, apart from the debarring of chestnut and coloured ponies, the only alteration was the setting of a

Roundthwaite Lucky Jim, aged twenty-one, champion Fell at the Ponies of Britain stallion show 1972.

height limit of 14 hands. There was no enforced minimum height and several ponies of 12.2 hh were registered at the time, although 13 hands was a more usual and recommended lower limit.

After the war, it was apparent to the Society that a new form of subsidised breeding scheme was necessary, as the traditional method of travelling stallions was now out of date and becoming increasingly ineffective. This was due to the fact that there were more Fell mares than before and they were distributed in a broad geographical area, fewer stallion owners were prepared to travel their entires, and there were not the financial resources to fund premiums in more than a handful of areas. The availability of transport in the form of trailers or horseboxes also answered the main difficulty that had given rise to the travelling stallion system in the first place. The solution was to run a breeding enclosure whereby members could turn their mares out on a tract of land set aside specially for the purpose with the stallion voted by members to run on the enclosure. Stallion owners were invited to offer their stallions for the enclosure and the stallion receiving the highest number of members' votes was awarded an enclosure premium of £30. The cost for mare owners was £2 and that covered the whole time she was on the enclosure, the season running from the end of May to the beginning of August. Mare owners had to apply to the secretary of the Society for an enclosure permit which, in those days, was only issued after the mare had been inspected for type and condition and passed. The first enclosure was run on a 100-acre piece of well-fenced and watered marginal land belonging to Mr Stanley Wilson at Berrier beneath Blencathra and Carrock Fell. Known as 'The Nettles', it was ideal for the purpose and Mr Wilson kept a watchful eye on the ponies, as did Mr Bell and Mr Winder who helped him. The Society ran two stallions on the enclosure in 1945, Linnel Raven for the first half of the season, and Linnel Romany II for the second half, although in subsequent years only one

Adamthwaite Lucky Star with visiting Fell mares on the Fell Pony Society's breeding enclosure at Berrier.

Mr W. S. Noble carrying on the tradition of the Heltondale herd in the 1980s with his champion homebred filly, Heltondale Maydew VII.

stallion ran on the enclosure for the whole season. The immediate success of the enclosure scheme convinced the Society that breeding enclosures should be arranged for future years. The system was inexpensive as one person could supervise all the ponies, and the percentage of mares leaving the enclosure in foal was very high.

In his annual report to the Society in 1948, the secretary wrote:

For the third consecutive year a very successful breeding scheme was carried out on Mr Wilson's ground at Berrier. The stallion used for the 1948 season was kindly lent by Mr J. Noble; this pony, Heltondale Roamer, is a good brown pony, well built with a pretty head and grand action; he was on the fells above Heltondale during the terrible winter of 1947, which alone proves the hardiness of the Fell breed. Only pedigree or approved Fell mares were accepted for the scheme and they received free grazing and a small premium to help to cover their travelling expenses to and from the enclosure. Altogether there were thirty-one mares at Berrier, coming from many localities in the Lake District, from Keswick to Tebay and Whitehaven, and from as far as Sussex, Hampshire and Sedbergh.

As demand increased, a second breeding enclosure was run at High Arnside, near Windermere, although this was later moved to Wet Sleddale and then to Dowthwaite Head above Ullswater. In 1950, eighteen mares were sent to the Berrier enclosure to run with Linnel Osprey, and seven went to run with Rowland Boy at Windermere. Sixteen years later, twenty-nine mares were sent to the enclosures, the following year it was forty-two mares altogether, and the next year it was up to forty-nine. The Fell Pony Society was the only breed society to run breeding enclosures, and they were largely responsible for reviving and restoring the breed after the ravages of two wars and a serious economic depression. In the early 1970s, the difficulty and expense of finding suitable land for enclosures, and the increasing preference of stallion owners to stand their entires at stud at home, started a fast decline in the popularity of enclosures. By 1976, the Society felt they were no longer viable and the scheme was discontinued. In its place, 'At Home' premiums were offered to stallions covering registered mares at home, so the premium grant from the Horserace Betting Levy Board (formerly the Racecourse Betting Control Board) was still being used for its original purpose but in a different way.

At the International Horse Show held at the White City, London, in 1948, the National Pony Society sponsored a parade of each of the mountain and moorland breeds of ponies. The Fell group was led by Linnel Romany II, a stallion bred by Mr R. B. Charlton whose death that year had been a great loss to the pony world in general. Other members of the group included Mr J. Bell's Bess O' The Hill with her filly foal, Mayflower O' The Hill, and Mrs McCosh's Dalemain Heather Bell. Over 3,000 people saw the Fell ponies on display over the five days of the show.

As well as his great interest in Fell ponies and the Society, the secretary, Mr Relph, was also known all over the country for his superb sheepdogs, Spy, Fleet and many others. During the 1940s, he was making films with his famous sheepdogs at Elstree Studios which were owned by Lady Gladys Yule. Mr Relph and Lady Yule often

A class for Fell ponies shown under saddle at a Cumberland show in the 1950s.

talked while he was working on the set, and she became very interested in both his dogs and his Fell ponies. Following a meeting with the assistant secretary, Mrs McCosh, Lady Yule felt she would like to help the Society and she did so by donating a cup for the best registered stallion. Soon afterwards she gave a youngstock cup to encourage the registration of progeny, and a third cup followed in due time. Lady Yule eventually became president of the Society and followed the interests of the breed to the end of her life.

91

Shap Lodge Duke, owned and ridden by Mrs A. Garcia of Devon, 1985.

At the Annual General Meeting in March 1950, the council discussed the recent announcement that the National Trust were disposing of their little herd of Fell ponies as the future of the breed was now sufficiently secure and the Trust was not constituted to keep livestock in normal times. The ponies were offered to the Fell Pony Society for a nominal sum, and the possibility of trying to keep the herd together was considered. In the end it was decided to sell the ponies to members of the Society at the 1950 Stallion and Colt Show. They were subsequently bought and dispersed throughout the north of England.

The discovery of riding as a recreational activity which started in the early 1950s and has gained momentum ever since gave all native breeds of ponies an opportunity to demonstrate their capabilities and qualities. It would ensure the survival of the breeds although it was still up to the breed societies to maintain the breed standard and see that important characteristics were not lost in the face of escalating demand for ponies. The decade was a sort of watershed for the Fell pony which had been essentially a general purpose work animal up until this point. Its future now lay in the field of leisure riding and driving, and to compete favourably with the other breeds and crosses it had to be versatile, adaptable and attractive to the general public.

7 The present-day Fell pony and its future

Up until the early 1950s, the Fell Pony Society had been very parochial. Its activities were all centred in the northwest of England where the breed had originated and where it was still found in concentrated numbers. Most of the members of the Society were resident in the north and, despite the publicity efforts of the Society, the breed was still largely unknown in other parts of the country.

With the increased interest in the breed at this time, mainly because the Fell ideally met the demand for strong, weight-carrying, docile and surefooted animals for the riding schools and trekking centres that were appearing everywhere in proliferation, the work load on the Society grew similarly. When the assistant secretary, Sylvia McCosh, resigned due to family commitments in 1955, her place was taken by Miss Peggy Crossland who carried on the work of helping the secretary, Mr Relph, with the job of dealing with the day-to-day secretarial work, registrations, membership applications, and running the breeding enclosures and stallion show. A few months later in February 1956 Mr Relph became ill and tragically died, and at the following Annual General Meeting Miss Crossland was elected secretary. Records for the

Miss Peggy Crossland, secretary of the Society from 1955 to 1981 and later president, presenting the supreme champion award to Mrs D. Slack's gelding, Townend Merlin, at the Fell Pony Society breed show 1983.

Society show that in 1956 there were eighty-six members and, during the year, twenty-five fillies and nineteen colts were registered. Twenty-five years later when Miss Crossland resigned and I became secretary, the membership had risen to 709 with 61 juniors, and 154 fillies and 110 colts were registered that year.

With the ultimate aim of improving the breed, a few new regulations were introduced during this period, one of the most effective being the grading-up scheme for the progeny of inspected ponies. The Society had run a very successful inspection scheme for ponies which were not registered and whose parentage was unknown and, encouraged by the National Pony Society, a system was devised and introduced in 1962 whereby the Fell pony stud book registrations were sub-divided into the following sections:

MAIN SECTION Containing ponies that have two fully registered parents.
INSPECTED Ponies that have only one registered parent, or an unknown pedigree, and have been inspected by the recognised Fell Pony Society Inspector.
SECTION A Filly foals from inspected mares by registered Fell stallions.
SECTION B Filly foals from section A mares by registered stallions. Their offspring by registered stallions were eligible for the main section (although if a colt, only after gelding).

On the registration certificates, the ponies carried the letters IS, A or B after their names to indicate the grading-up section they belonged to. Colts out of any but main section mares were only eligible for registration after they had been gelded. At the spring council meeting in February 1969, it was decided to close the stud book to all but registered and graded-up ponies, and the following year the inspection scheme ended. Many felt this was a retrograde step as there would still be many good ponies which had never been registered running out on the fells, but the Society decided it had given owners ample opportunity to get their stock registered.

In order to be eligible for an increase in the Horserace Betting Levy Board grant, administered on their behalf by the National Pony Society, the Society was persuaded to insist that *all* stallions were licensed by the Ministry of Agriculture, as opposed only to those standing at public stud. This entailed a veterinary inspection to ensure that the stallions were free from hereditary unsoundness, but it did not guarantee that ponies were of correct Fell type. With this in mind, a colt inspection scheme was introduced in the early 1970s and all colts had to be inspected by three selected judges from the Fell Pony Society judge's panel. Only those colts which passed this inspection could go on to be vetted for a ministry licence. As an encouragement, the Society made a grant payment towards the cost of getting each colt licensed. This system continued until the early 1980s when dissatisfaction with the inspection scheme prompted the Society to drop it. With the demise of the Ministry of Agriculture licensing system, the Society began to issue its own stallion licences in 1983. To obtain a licence, the pony had to be vetted by a veterinary surgeon other than the pony owner's own vet, and the completed form, issued by the Society, had to be returned to the secretary who prepared and forwarded the actual licensing certificate. When the licensing of stallions was originally introduced, stallions used only on the owner's own mares were exempt as some breeders who kept their ponies on the fell in a semi-feral state complained that it would have been difficult for them to get their stallions in and handled for the veterinary inspection. Now, all breeding stallions must be licensed as foals can only be registered if their sire has a licence. Although this does not ensure standards of conformation, action or type, the system is self-regulating as, with plenty of ponies about as opposed to the limited numbers of earlier decades, breeders are unlikely to keep a poor quality entire when there are better ponies available. The improved quality of stallions in recent years would validate this theory.

All registrations continued to be recorded in the Fell section of the National Pony Society stud book up until 1980, when the Society decided that it should print its own annual stud books quite independently of the National Pony Society. The old system meant that registration applications came to the Fell Pony Society for checking before being sent on to the National Pony Society for recording and typing of the registration certificate. The system was long-winded and would become more so as the number of annual registrations and transfers of ownership increased. The financial implications made it increasingly unattractive as two societies were necessarily involved with each registration, which was expensive in terms of staff time and postage, and people wanting a copy of Fell registrations were compelled to buy the National Pony Society stud book for the given year which also included the registrations for the other native breeds as well as riding ponies. The first Fell Pony Society stud book was published in 1981 and subsequent editions have been brought out annually ever since.

With only minor amendments, the constitution of the Fell Pony Society has virtually remained unchanged since the early years of the Society. The object has always been 'to foster and keep pure the old breed of pony which has roamed the northern fells for years and to circulate knowledge and general information about the breed'. The management of the Society is conducted by a council of twenty members, four of whom retire each year in rotation but are eligible for re-election at the Annual General Meeting. New nominations for the council must be made to the secretary at least eight weeks before the Annual General Meeting. In addition, a president is elected at the same meeting each March to hold office for a period of two years. A president elect is chosen half way through the president's term of office so as to ensure continuity, and a chairman and vice chairman are elected annually from the council. The president and president elect, like the secretary/treasurer, are ex-officio voting members of the council. Council meetings are held in February and September, the Annual General Meeting in March, and the Autumn General Meeting in October.

Fell pony stallion, Townend Flash IV, owned by Mrs J. Brownrigg and ridden sidesaddle by Miss Rose Brundrett.

The Society holds a stallion and colt show at Penrith each May with classes for registered yearlings, two year olds, stallions three or four years old, and senior stallions five years and over. A class for ridden stallions was successfully introduced some years ago, and more recently a class for driven stallions was included. Acknowledging the importance of a good foot on a Fell pony, a class for the best foot shod was added to the schedule, and a rule was later passed that to be eligible for an 'At Home' premium a stallion had to be paraded at the stallion show so that mare owners could see him in the flesh and in comparison to the other entires there. Bearing in mind that in the early years of the Society stallions were led to the stallion show and consequently were drawn from a very local catchment area, the show has grown enormously, with exhibitors travelling from all parts of the country to compete for the premiums with their ponies. There has been a marked improvement

A young competitor riding a Fell pony in a junior show jumping class, 1979.

in the quality and consistency of ponies over the last two decades with fewer poorer quality animals standing down the line.

Since the early 1970s, the Society has held a summer breed show at Penrith each August. The early shows were comparatively modest affairs with a limited schedule of classes, but as showing has increased in popularity the show has grown annually until it is now one of the largest shows catering for an individual breed in the country. The wide range of classes include those for all ages of fillies, mares, colts and geldings in hand, stallion and mare progeny groups, ridden classes for novice and open mares and geldings, ridden veterans for ponies eighteen years or over, children's riding classes, handy pony, working hunter, private driving and obstacle driving, fancy dress, best foot shod, best foot unshod, plus in recent years a qualifying class for the National Pony Society Ridden Mountain and Moorland Championship. Each year the show gets a little bigger, which is an encouraging sign for the Society. In order to cater for the many Fell pony enthusiasts in the south, a Southern Fell Pony Breed Show was held for the first time in September 1989, and other smaller Fell pony shows, held under the auspices of the Society, have been arranged in other parts of the country.

The importance of showing the versatility of the breed is something the Society has always been aware of. In 1980 the first Fell pony performance trial was held at Packway, the Windermere home of Miss Peggy Crossland, and its success soon established it as an annual event. The course was laid out on a twenty-four acre allotment behind the house and comprised a series of obstacles such as one might meet on a ride across the fells. Ponies were marked on the way they negotiated steep and difficult gradients often winding between rocks and trees, forded streams, picked their way through boggy ground, traversed fallen trees, and generally behaved while their riders coped with opening and shutting gates mounted and performed other tasks intended to demonstrate the handiness and responsiveness of the pony. A little later, a second annual performance trial held in the spring of the year was introduced, and this was run on the lines of a one-day event with dressage, cross country and show jumping phases. When the Society was allocated a qualifying round for the National Pony Society Mountain and Moorland Working Hunter Championship at Malvern, it was decided to hold it at the Rydal Spring Performance Trial and, as with the Olympia final, those ponies which qualified represented the breed with credit and frequently were among the prizewinners. Building on the success of these prestigious finals, which have done so much to encourage the use of British native breeds in a performance capacity, a Mountain and Moorland Driving

Miss R. Freeman riding Drimla Dale on the cross country course at the 1984 Rydal Performance Trials.

A competitor taking part in one of the performance trials organised by the Society to demonstrate the capabilities of the breed.

Mr Jack Marsden's Dene Claudius, winner of the National Pony Society Mountain and Moorland Driving Championship, Malvern, 1989.

Championship was instigated by the National Pony Society later on and, again, the representatives of the Fell breed acquitted themselves well and won the championship on more than one occasion.

Since 1901, the annual Wigton horse sale, held each October at Wigton in Cumbria, has included a section for Fell ponies. When the Society decided that an official sale of registered ponies should be held each year, Wigton was chosen as the ideal venue and to this day the Society holds its official sale of stock in conjunction with the Wigton auctioneers. For a number of years the sale has been preceded by a show to encourage buyers and help publicise the correct type of pony. Fell ponies were also frequently sold at the famous Cowper Day sale held at Kirkby Stephen each year at the end of September. In 1960, the first prize winning pony at the official sale was a two-year-old filly and she sold for the excellent price of £52. The second prize pony, an eight-year-old brown mare, made £39. A five-year-old ride and drive mare made £50, with yearling fillies at £29 and £35, and yearling geldings £21 and £22. Considerably more interest was being shown in geldings as the prices reflected, and a two-year-old black gelding made £32. Seven years later, an eleven-year-old in-foal mare made the top price of £130, and a seven-year-old gelding, quiet to ride, made £105. In 1968, the top price was £145 for a black three-year-old in-foal mare. Twenty years later, yearling and two-year-old geldings were making in excess of £400 while a broken mare sold for over £800. Even with these encouraging prices, the demand for good ponies, especially older broken animals, was reducing the number of ponies put up for auction at the official sale as vendors could sell their stock privately with little trouble. Private transactions have been responsible for some enormous prices in recent years.

With the popularity of showing generally and more shows including classes for Fell ponies in their schedules, the need for more and more judges with the required knowledge to judge these ponies grew. The Fell Pony Society was very aware that the popularity of showing could have a great influence on the breed as those ponies which won in the showring would be seen as the model of excellence for the breed, and exhibitors would aim to produce that particular type. If judges were not really aware of what constituted a good Fell pony, their poor judging could set trends which would ruin the breed. With this in mind, the Society maintained a list of carefully selected and approved judges, copies of which were sent to show secretaries and organisers. Realising the importance of encouraging young judges and instilling in them the necessary knowledge and experience to do their work competently, a junior judging class was arranged for young members sixteen years and under at the summer breed show. From this humble beginning, the trainee judges scheme was formulated whereby people of any age with a real interest in the breed would be given the opportunity to train as a judge by learning alongside an experienced judge at shows with Fell pony classes. Trainees would attend a designated number of shows for a set period of time at the end of which, subject to favourable reports from the master judges, the trainee progressed to an assistant judge then, with ratification from the council, as a fully fledged Fell pony judge. The scheme is always over-subscribed with applicants, which is a healthy sign for the future.

Fell owners are encouraged to exhibit their ponies in classes for mixed native breeds at shows all over the country by the awarding by the Fell Pony Society of Fell special rosettes to the highest placed Fell in ridden, in-hand, driven or working

HRH The Princess of Wales being welcomed to the Fell Pony Society exhibition stand at the 1988 Royal Show by Mr J. Wykes and Mrs S. Hardy.

hunter classes. As well as being an encouragement to owners, the rosette scheme helps to draw attention to Fell ponies in mixed breed classes.

An exhibition stand manned voluntarily by members of the Society and promoting the breed is taken to many of the national equestrian shows and events, and breed publicity leaflets are distributed at displays and shows to the general public who enquire about the Fell. Members are kept informed of the Society's activities, forthcoming events, and general news about the breed by the circulation of bi-annual illustrated newsletters. The breed's interests elsewhere are represented by delegates who attend the meetings of other equestrian organisations on the Society's behalf and report back to council meetings.

Inevitably, the growth of interest in the breed nationally led, in time, to interest being shown from abroad, and although Fells had been exported previously with the purpose of improving the native stock in Spain, Pakistan and elsewhere, the export enquiries now were for Fells in their own right. In 1947, Linnel Sandpiper, a black

Mr and Mrs L. Nygaard's Lowmoat Samson, two-year-old colt, exported to the USA in 1988 as foundation stock for the first Fell pony stud in America.

Two-year-old Fells owned by Mr and Mrs L. Nygaard of Florida: *(above)* Tarnbeck Lightning,
colt bred by Mrs G. Williamson; *(below)* Waverhead Bonny, filly bred by Mr J. Bell.

three-year-old filly bred by Mr Charlton, made the long journey to Melbourne, Australia, and the same year Mrs McCosh sold a three-year-old colt to a buyer in Northern India.

Three years later, the Society received an enquiry from Herr Hirsch, a German official, who wanted to import 5,000 strong ponies not of show standard to work the sandy soiled farms in Western Germany where machinery was difficult and expensive to obtain. He was able to offer £20 per pony which the Society thought insufficient and the deal never materialised. It was not until some years later that a number of Fells were exported to Germany for riding and driving.

However, an enquiry from America led to the first Fell ponies crossing the Atlantic in 1934 when Mr Charlton sold Linnel Frivolity, Linnel Tinker and Monks Bess to a lady in Virginia. A stallion was sold to some people in South Carolina at the same time. A few years later, Dalemain Bluebell, a three-year-old filly bred by Mrs McCosh, went to a new home in Virginia, and Dalemain Foxglove followed her soon after. Both Dalemain ponies ended their days as shooting ponies in Louisiana.

More recently, five Fells were exported to Florida where it is hoped they will form the foundation stock for the first Fell stud in North America.

During the 1960s, a number of Fell ponies were imported into Canada by Mr E. P. Taylor, the bloodstock owner and breeder of the famous racehorse, Nijinsky. He used them to establish a small stud producing pure Fells and Thoroughbred crosses.

Individual ponies were also exported to a number of European countries including France, Germany and Holland, and one mare bred by the Greenfield Stud in Yorkshire was flown out to Israel to be used by a disabled rider on a kibbutz.

Before assessing the present-day Fell pony, the Society's official standard of excellence for which is given below, it is worth remembering how little the breed has changed over the centuries since its establishment in post-Roman times. It is highly probable that modern breeders transported back in time twelve or more centuries would recognise the Fell pony of the time as the same breed they know today. In commending its purity, R. S. Summerhays said that he believed the Fell 'had in it as little alien blood as any' and other writers spoke of the Fell's consistency of type in generation after generation. It is interesting to compare how similar the following current description of the breed is to that written by Mr Wingate-Saul nearly a century ago:

DESCRIPTION OF FELL PONY AND SCALE OF POINTS

HEIGHT Not exceeding fourteen hands.

COLOUR Black, brown, bay and grey, preferably with no white markings though a star or a little white on the foot is allowed.

HEAD Small, well chiselled in outline, well set on, forehead broad, tapering to nose.

NOSTRILS Large and expanding.

EYES Prominent, bright, mild and intelligent.

EARS Neatly set, well formed and small.

THROAT AND JAWS Fine, showing no sign of throatiness nor coarseness.

NECK Of proportionate length, giving good length of rein, strong and not too heavy, moderate crest in case of stallion.

SHOULDERS Most important, well laid back and sloping, not too fine at withers, nor loaded at the points – a good long shoulder blade, muscles well developed.

CARCASE Good strong back of good outline, muscular loins, deep carcase, thick through heart, round ribbed from shoulders to flank, short and well coupled, hind quarters square and strong with tail well set on.

FEET, LEGS AND JOINTS Feet of good size, round and well formed, open at heels with the characteristic blue horn, fair sloping pasterns not too long, fore-legs should be straight, well placed not tied at elbows, big well formed knees, short cannon bone, plenty of good flat bone below knee, eight inches at least, great muscularity of arm.

HIND LEGS Good thighs and second thighs, very muscular, hocks well let down and clean cut, plenty of bone below joint, hocks should not be sickle nor cow hocked.

MANE, TAIL AND FEATHER Plenty of fine hair at heels (coarse hair objectionable), all the fine hair except that at point of heel may be cast in summer. Mane and tail are left to grow long.

ACTION Walk, smart and true. Trot well balanced all round with good knee and hock action, going well from the shoulder and flexing the hocks, not going too wide nor near behind. Should show great pace and endurance, bringing the hind legs well under the body when going.

GENERAL CHARACTER The Fell pony should be constitutionally as hard as iron and show good pony characteristics with the unmistakable appearance of hardiness peculiar to mountain ponies and, at the same time, have a lively and alert appearance and great bone.

107

Height and colour	5 points
Head, nostrils, eyes, ears, throat, jaws, neck	10 points
Shoulders	15 points
Carcase	20 points
Feet, legs and joints, and hind legs	25 points
Action	25 points
General characteristics	100 points

A good Fell should be a substantial animal, well built and powerful but active and free moving, with plenty of pony quality and native character. There was a trend in the late 1940s and early 1950s to divide the breed into two quite distinct types, an old-fashioned type of heavier pony, and a lighter riding type. It was a misguided idea as

the true Fell pony is an excellent ride despite its weight-carrying build. R. S. Summerhays, the horseman and writer, wrote: 'a well trained Fell makes a delightful ride for his activity, strength and hardiness, born of generations of scrambling about the mountains, give him great balance and what horse is worth riding without this?' Assessing his weaknesses, he added: 'he lacks a certain grace of bearing found in some of the other breeds. I believe him to be the ideal family pony for he can carry a heavy man with ease and with his temperament he may be trusted with children.' The idea of two types within the breed was even supported by the Fell Pony Society for a time and, when they began operating two breeding enclosures, it was decided to run a stallion of the heavier type at High Arnside and a stallion of riding type at Berrier. Consequently, Rowland Boy was turned out at High Arnside and Linnel Osprey at Berrier. Fragmentation within any breed invariably results in a weakening of

Consistency of type over sixty years: *(opposite page)* Moor Bradley, owned and bred by J. Bellas, Keswick, first prize winner at the National Pony Society show, London, 1928; *(below)* Greenfield Gay Lad, shown by his owner Mr C. Howarth, champion at the Fell Pony Society stallion show 1987.

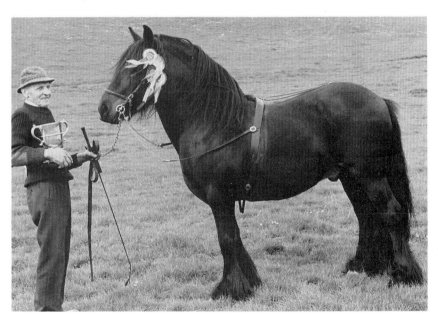

standards, and the realisation that the old-fashioned type of pony could also be a good ride and could jump and go in harness came in time to stop the breed deteriorating as a result. Ill-conceived attempts to improve breeds by making them larger or stronger or whatever to suit short-term demands have resulted in the loss of many breeds including the Galloway pony, when it is quite feasible that the true original type could have adequately met all purposes. Considering that the Fell was developed as a draught and pack animal in the first place, it is commendable that it is now essentially a riding pony, capable of galloping and jumping, and yet it has lost none of its original type nor had to compromise any of its true characteristics.

Over the years breeders have tried to tamper with the Fell's naturally straight ground-covering action. R. S. Summerhays commented that as the Fell had 'been bred for generations to walk and to trot at a great pace, this makes exaggerated knee action impossible'. However, it did not prevent tradesmen in the last century from

Mrs Charlotte Johnson riding Barncrosh Brandy in a cross country event.

training Fells to high-step by means of lead weights, pulleys or hardwood 'rattlers' fastened around the ponies' pasterns. It was felt that this artificial action was flashy and eye-catching and would attract customers' attention. It was achieved at the cost of length of stride, and purists decried it as wasteful as the pony moved energetically but covered little ground. High knee action also makes a pony uncomfortable to ride and therefore limits its suitability for a variety of purposes. Back in the thirteenth and fourteenth centuries, north-country farmers had often specialised in the breeding and training of Fell ponies which they then sold to wealthy townsmen and gentry as suitable mounts for long journeys. The significant feature of these ponies was their economical long-striding action, which made them comfortable to ride for long distances as well as relatively fast. They were always ridden at a walk or trot and, in old wills, records, inventories and documents of the time, they were often referred to as 'rakkers' or 'raks', although the term was loosely used to refer to riding animals of different types which either trotted or paced. In the north a 'rakker' generally signified an easy moving and comfortable riding animal. The importance of avoiding excessive knee action in the Fell was something the Fell Pony Committee for Cumberland, Westmorland and North Yorkshire was aware of and, at their spring meeting in 1916, they agreed that it would be a mistake to encourage Hackney-type action. They were evidently concerned about the success of Christopher Wilson's Hackney ponies from nearby Rigmaden Park which had originally been developed from Fell pony crosses. Had other people tried to emulate Wilson's success by crossing their valuable Fell brood mares with other breeds to produce animals with more action, the breed would have suffered considerably. The committee agreed that crossing with Wilson ponies must be discouraged as 'they had too much Hackney character for local needs'.

The popularity of showing has had a number of indirect influences on the breed. Black has become the most fashionable colour in the showring and now more ponies are registered of this colour than of the other three permissible colours. Grey, which is an old Fell colour, is least popular as grey Fells are occasionally inadvertently mistaken for other breeds in the showring and some people mistakenly feel that black is more typical for the breed. Modern preference is for black ponies and since this colour is recessive to bay, brown or grey it is possible that these other colours may become gradually rarer over the years and even lost to the breed altogether.

Similarly, showring preferences have reduced the percentage of ponies being registered with white markings. The rules and regulations of the Fell Pony Society state that any pony is eligible for registration provided both its parents are fully

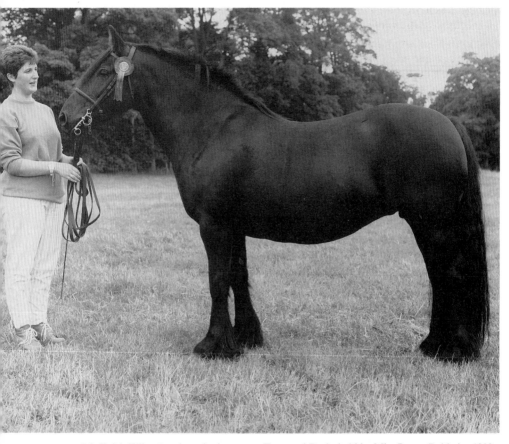

Mr E. M. Wilson's prize-winning mare, Townend Ruth, held by Miss Penny Baldwin, 1989.

registered, and that the foal is either black, brown, bay or grey. White markings are allowed, although anything more than a small white star or a little white on the back feet is discouraged as it indicates possible cross breeding somewhere in the pony's ancestry.

The height limit for the breed stands at 14 hands with half an inch allowed for shoes. Many breeders believe that the height should never have been raised above

13.2 hh, which is what it was for many years, while others are in favour of raising it above 14 hands. It is quite likely that the Fell has benefited from raising the height limit two inches as this has increased its scope by making it more attractive as a riding pony for adults and as a performance animal in shows and events in competition with ponies of the other native breeds. The danger lies in losing the breed type and character by altering the breed standard, and it would undoubtedly be a retrograde step to consider changing the height limit or any of the other breed criteria now when the Fell has proved itself capable of fulfilling the demands of today's discriminating market.

Inevitably, some ponies will grow over height. In most cases, this is due to moving the ponies from their natural environment on to better quality grassland where they do better and grow faster. From earliest times, the size of the Fell pony was dictated by the type of ground it roamed over and the quality and abundance of the vegetation it found to live on. An animal of 15 hands would never have survived a hard winter on the bleak Lakeland fells. By rigidly enforcing the height limit, the Fell Pony Society ensures that conformity within the breed is maintained and that ponies bred in other parts of the country or even abroad are not significantly different from those bred in the north of England. As ponies are usually registered as foals, there is no guarantee that as adult animals they may not grow too big. To exert some control over this potential situation, a system exists whereby the owners of up to height animals exhibited in the showring may be asked to get their ponies measured officially under the Joint Measurement Scheme. If the animal measures in, the measuring fee is paid for by the Society. However, if the pony measures out, the fee is paid by the owner and the certificate of registration is invalidated. This system, which discourages the showing of any animal which is too big, has proved to be self-regulating as its existence has virtually made its implementation unnecessary. At the same time, it does not penalise owners of large mares kept for breeding only and which, put to a smaller stallion, may breed something well within the specified height limit.

The suggestion of having a utility section in the stud books for registered, over-height animals which would be permitted to compete in performance events and classes only was voted down by the Society. Had it been approved, it would have encouraged a division within the breed, given approval by registration to ponies which did not conform to the breed standard, and intimated that over-height ponies were better suited to performance work. The establishment of a utility section, like that of a part-bred register which has also been suggested at various times, would necessitate a reappraisal of the Society's objectives and a rewriting of the

Mr P. Forsman's eighteen-year-old mare, Bowderdale Jess, ridden by Miss Susan Forsman, 1989.

constitution which states that the Society's aim is to foster and keep pure the Fell pony.

With so many and varied competitive opportunities for native ponies, the standard of turnout and schooling has improved tremendously over the past few years but must never be allowed to overshadow the importance of conformation, action and type. The standard of presentation, particularly for winter shows, is often achieved by clipping and rugging and other artificial means but, at the end of the day, native ponies should look like native ponies. Moreover, in theory at least, they should be capable of being roughed off after a show and returned to their natural environment, or the true mountain and moorland character of these ponies will be lost and a separate 'show type' of animal will evolve.

Every year the percentage of Fell ponies bred on the fells of northern England decreases as the number of ponies bred and kept in other parts of the country increases. A wider distribution of the breed, both nationally and abroad, has to be a good thing but success brings its own problems and the overwhelming demand for Fells, particularly older broken ponies, must not permit a compromise in standards. In future years, the Fell Pony Society is more likely to be working to ensure the survival of the breed standard than, as was once the case, to prevent the breed from dying out altogether. Responsibility for the Fell pony in years to come really lies in the hands of breeders, enthusiasts, judges and anyone else connected with the breed. After nearly two centuries of tumultuous history which has seen many changes and threats to the breed, the Fell pony is now in a stronger position in terms of purebred population and overall quality than ever before. On this basis, optimism for the future would seem justified and an important part of our north-country heritage will be preserved for future generations to enjoy.

Bibliography

Alderson, Lawrence. *Rare breeds*. Shire Publications, 1984

Charlton, Roy. *A lifetime with ponies*. Hexham Abbey Press, 1944

Cobbett, William. *Rural rides*. 1830; repr. Constable, 1982

Dent, A. A. *Lost beasts of Britain*. Harrap, 1974

Dent, A. A. and Machin Goodall, D. *The foals of Epona*. Galley Press, 1962.
  Reprinted as *A history of British native ponies*. J. A. Allen, 1988

Fiennes, Celia. *The journeys of Celia Fiennes*. Repr. Macdonald, 1983

Gilbey, Sir Walter. *Thoroughbred and other ponies*. Vinton, 1903

Richardson, Clive. *The Fell pony*. Dalesman, 1981

Ryder, Tom. *The high stepper*. J. A. Allen, 1961

Summerhays, R. S. *The observer's book of horses and ponies*. Warne & Co., 1949

Wilson, J. *A Cumbrian blacksmith*. Dalesman, 1978

Youatt, William. *The different breeds of English horses*. c. 1820

Youatt, William. *The horse*. Baldwin, 1851

Fell Pony Society archives: articles, letters and records
National Pony Society stud books, 1898–1980

Index

Page numbers in italics refer to illustrations